Morte d'Arthur

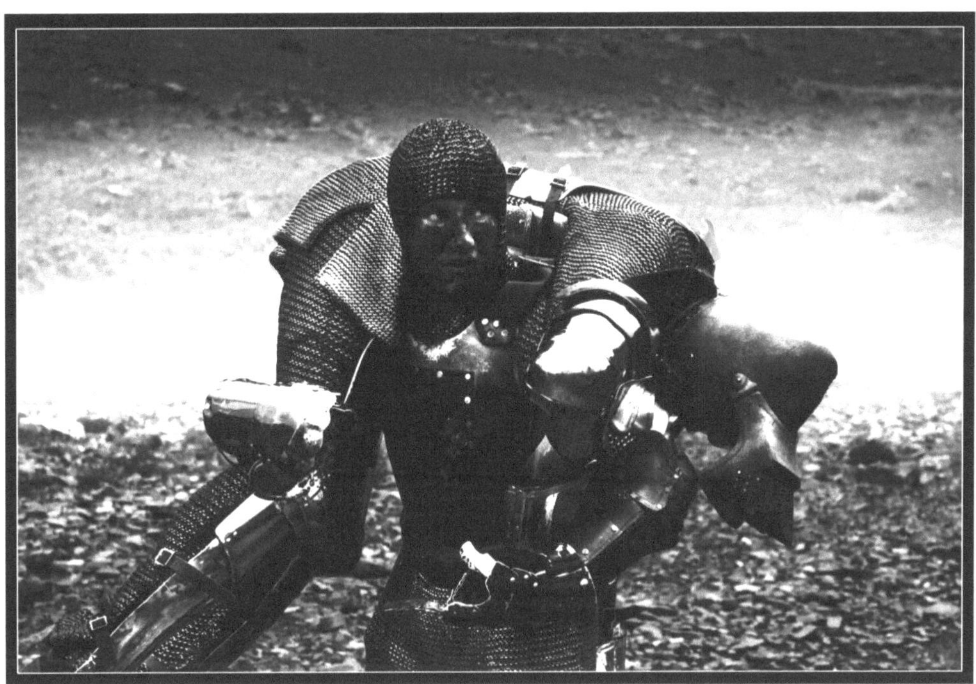

Morte d'Arthur

A Photographic Representation

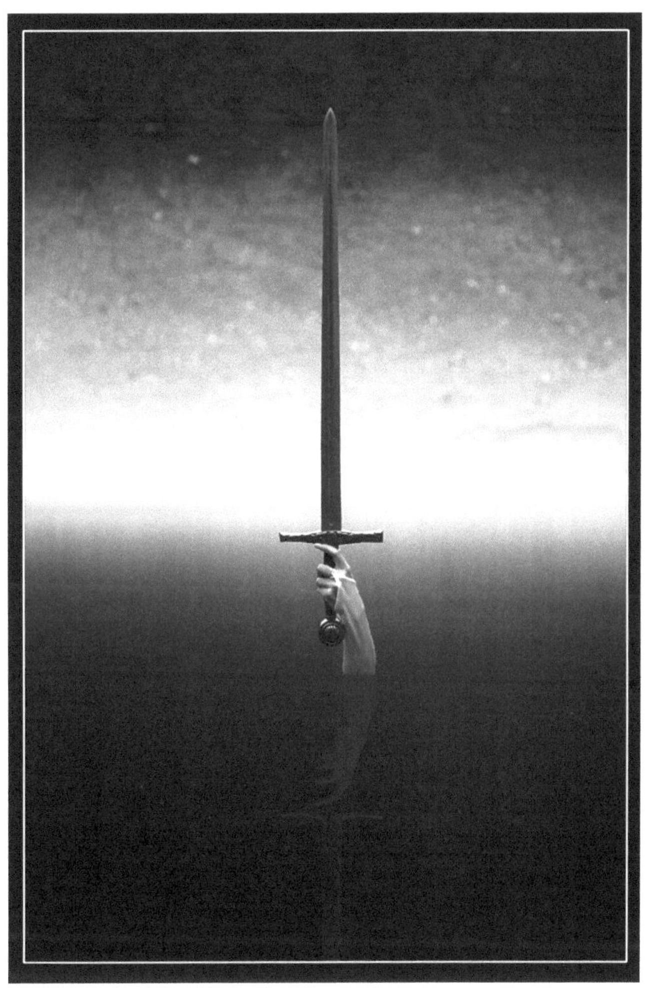

Neil Collier

First published 2008

ISBN 978-0-9558487-0-4

Designed by Neil Collier

www.neilcollierphotography.co.uk

Contents

Introduction

"King Arthur". From a young age I have always loved the romance and chivalry that surround these two words. I have always been facinated at the prospect of an individual who champions the causes of the innocent, and strives to combat evil. In reality, and with maturity of age, I have realised the world is not a perfect place, but one cannot easily take from you your own childhood dreams, ideals and visions derived from descriptive texts.
The first time I read 'Morte d'Arthur' was when I was twenty-three years old. Late in life you may think, but I had never been provided the opportunity to read the works of Tennyson. A lengthy poem it is, but during the first few lines my imagination painted vivid images of knights in armour and King Arthur himself; in a sad way of course, but still with a vision of grandeur.
Not long afterwards I started to sketch outlines for the scenes which would eventually become the visualisation which you are about to see.
From start to finish the project took around three years to complete, from the first sketches to the opening night of the exhibition.
While some individuals may disagree with me, I believe that photography is an art form and can be used to great effect in many creative ways. I cannot draw or paint very well so I use light as my medium, and the camera as my instrument of choice.

Let the journey begin...

Neil Collier

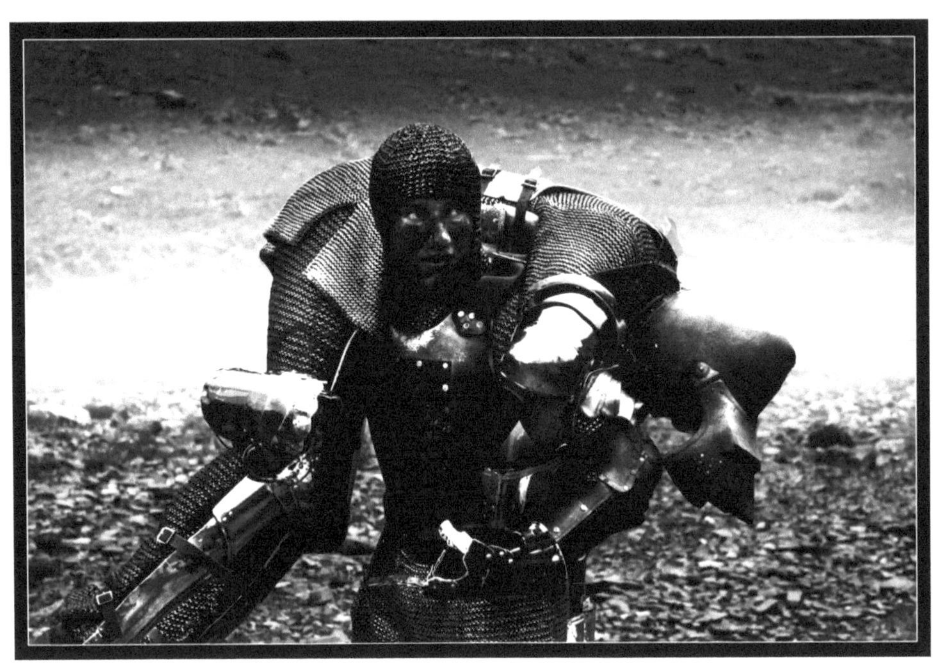

This book is dedicated to Mike and Barbara my Parents,
Kevin, and my Fiancé, Emma.

Valiant people in their own right.

also,
to Grant, Helen, Martin, Sillé, Wendy, Laura,
Kim, Kath and the staff of The King Arthur Hotel.
Without their support this project would never have been completed.

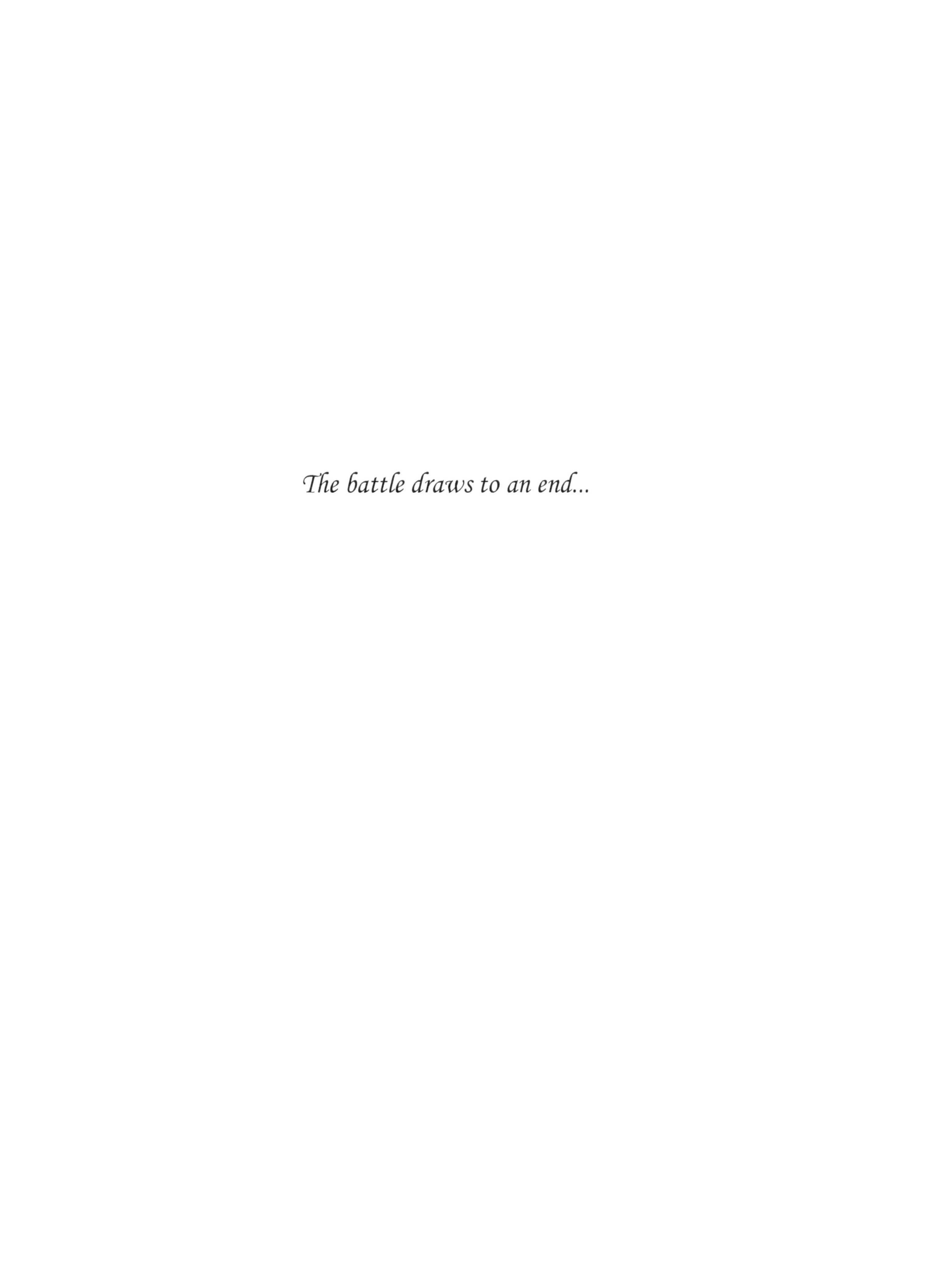

The battle draws to an end...

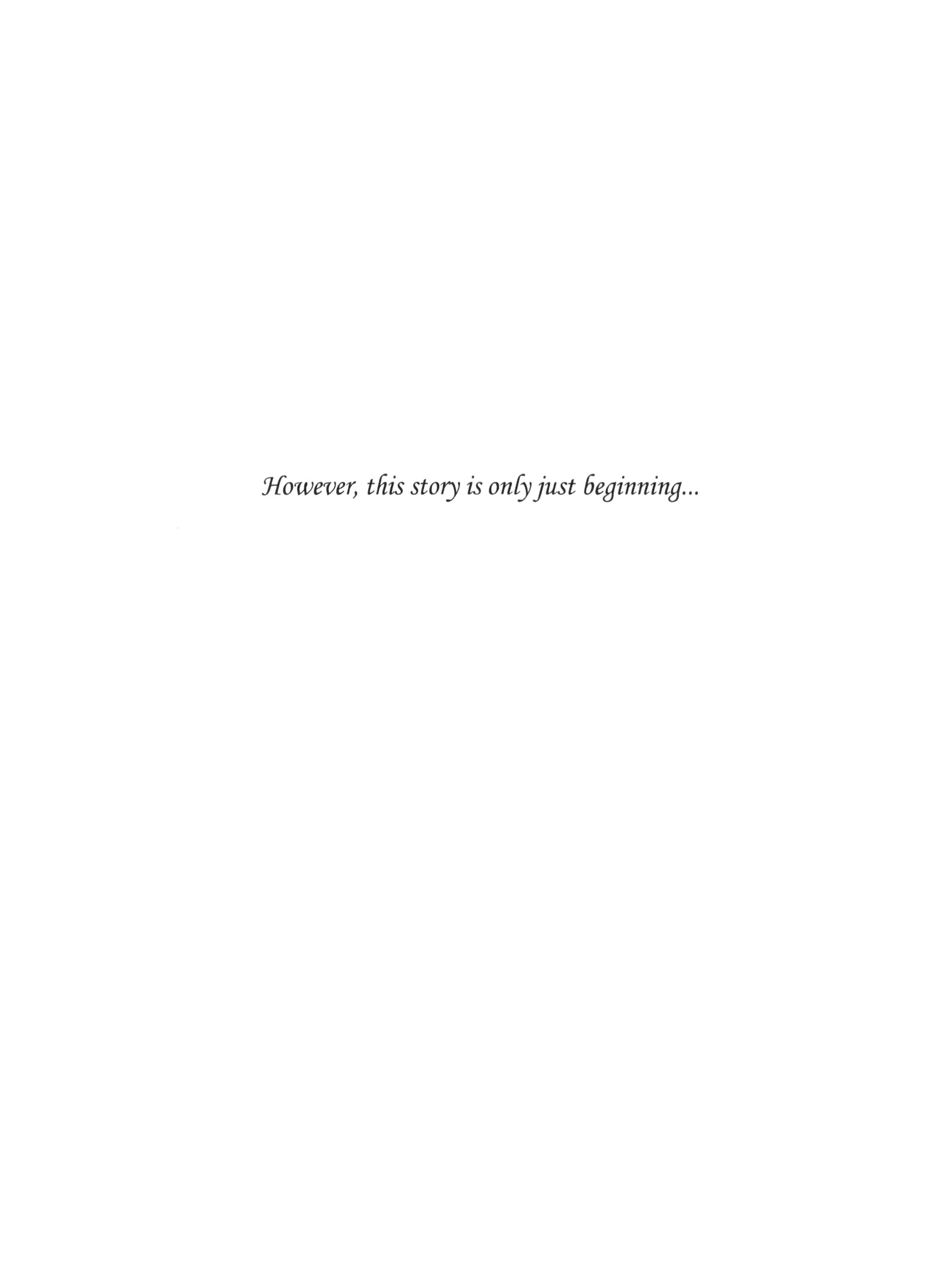

However, this story is only just beginning...

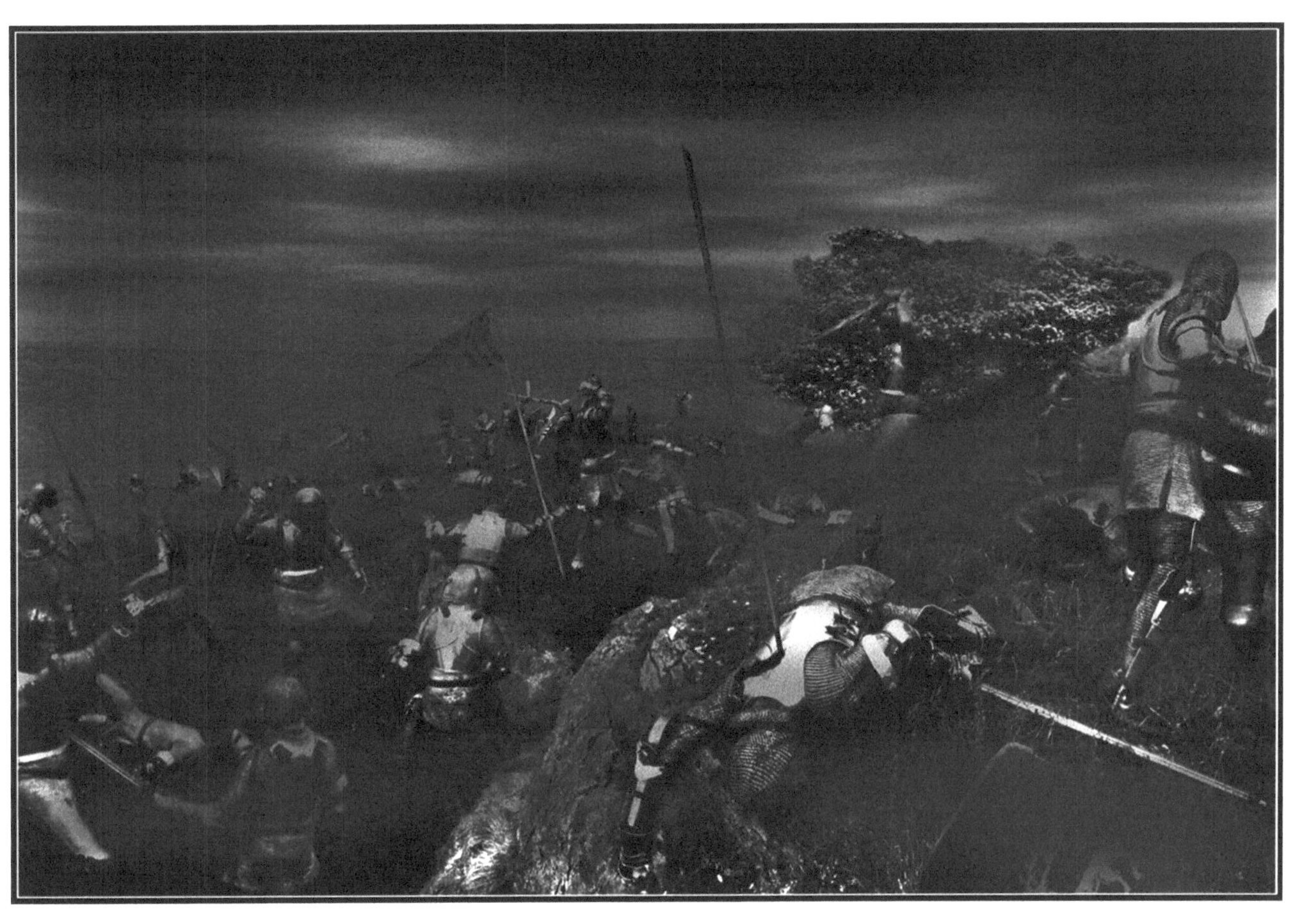

So all day long the noise of battle roll'd
Among the mountains by the winter sea;
Until King Arthur's table, man by man,
Had fallen in Lyonnesse about their Lord,

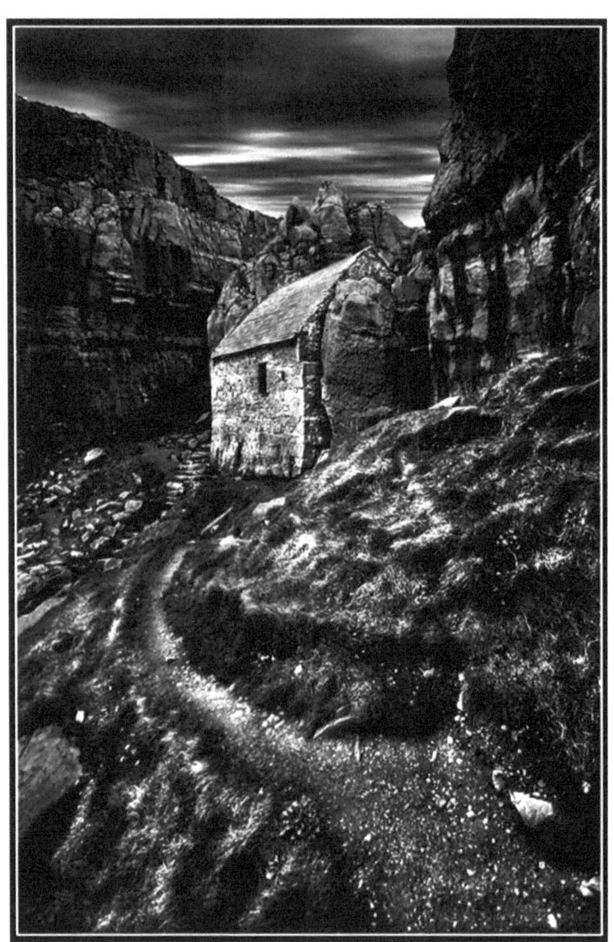

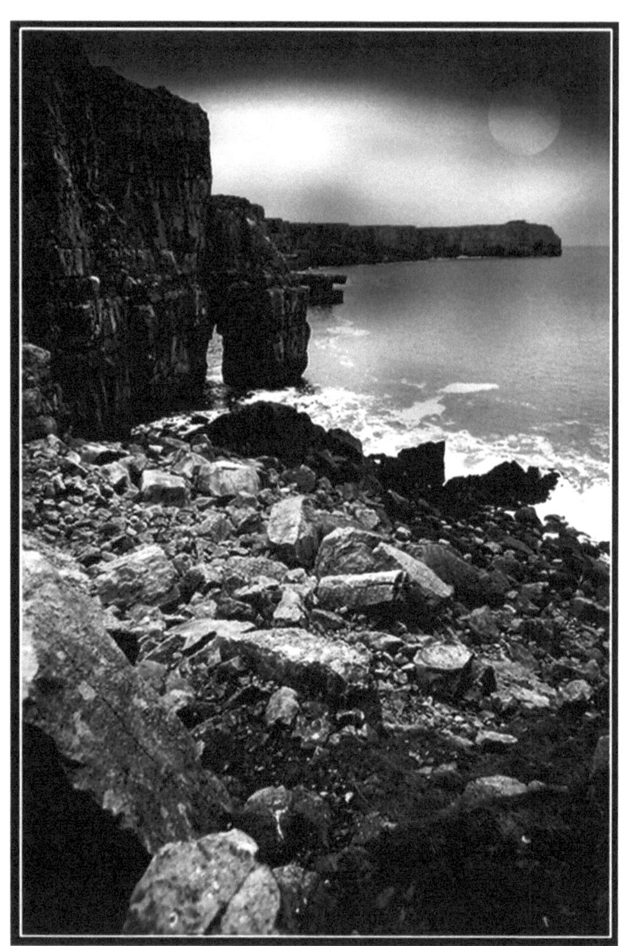

King Arthur: then, because his wound was deep,
The bold Sir Bedivere uplifted him,
Sir Bedivere, the last of all his Knights,
And bore him to a chapel nigh the field,
A broken chancel with a broken cross,
That stood on a dark strait of barren land.
On one side lay the Ocean, and on one
Lay a great water, and the moon was full.

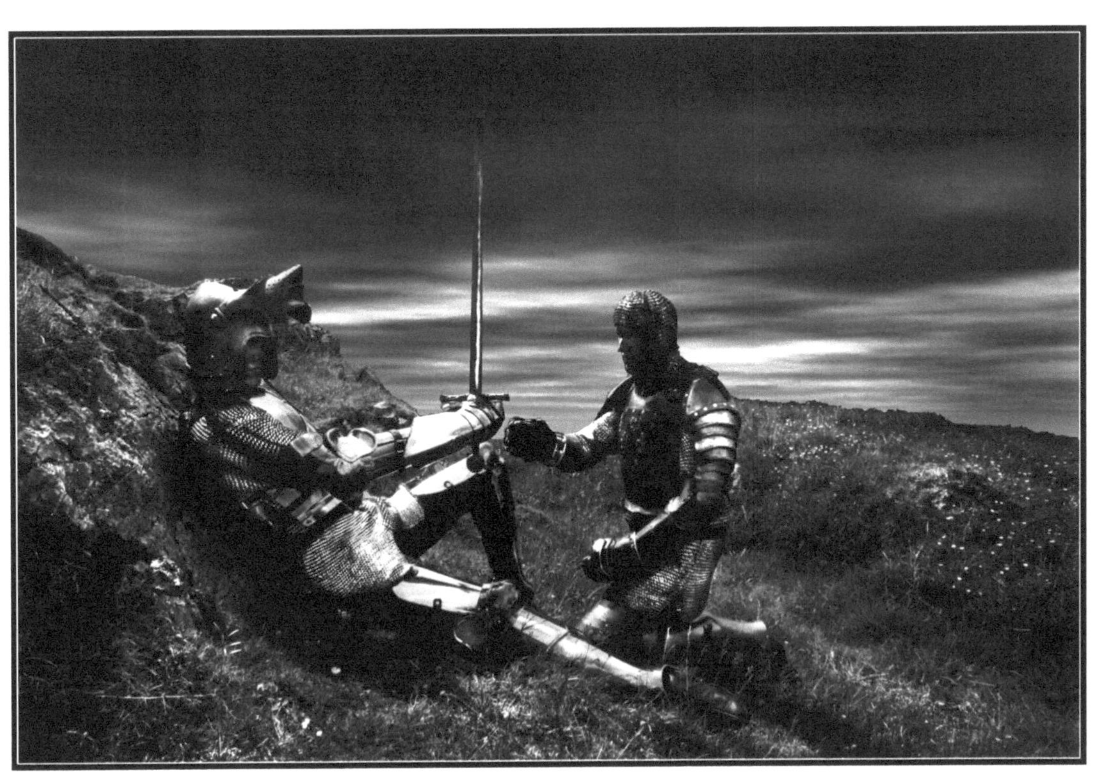

I am so deeply smitten thro' the helm
That without help I cannot last till morn.

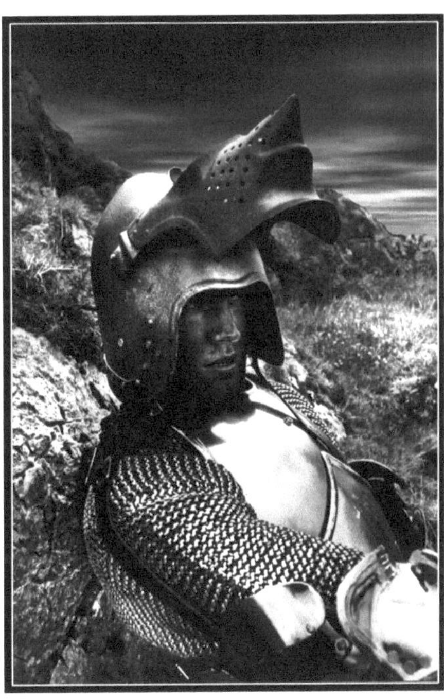

Thou therefore take my brand Excalibur,
Which was my pride:

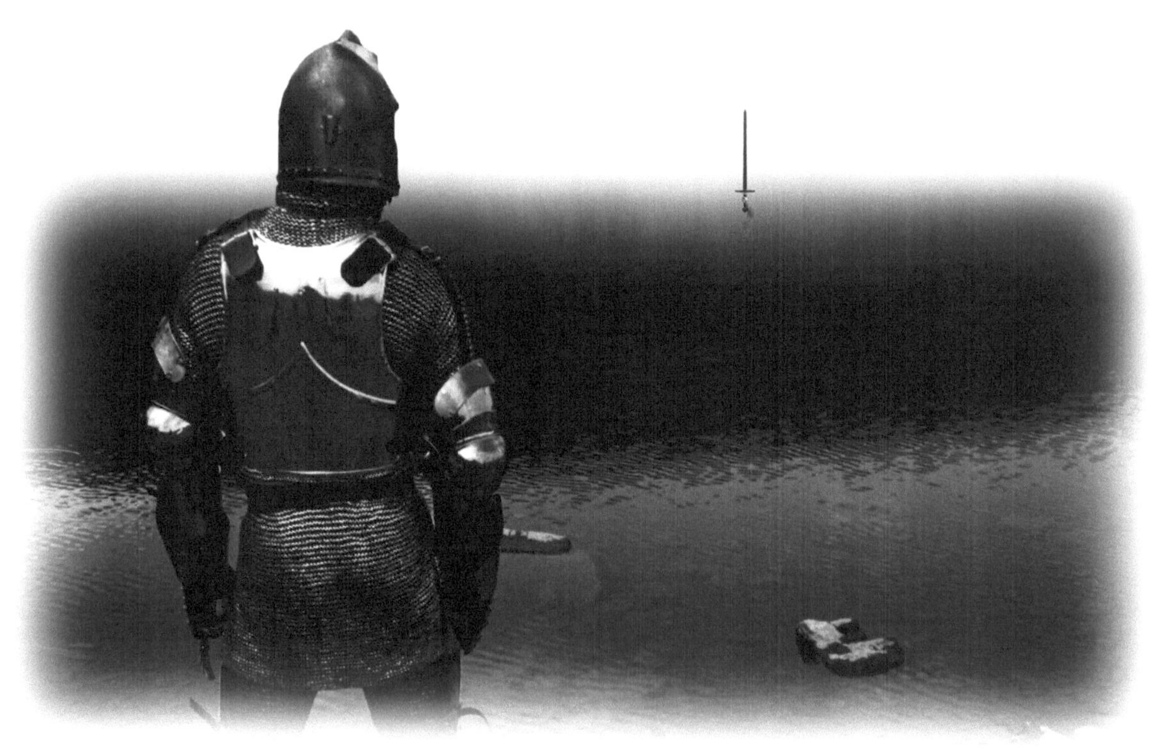

for thou rememberest how
In those old days, one summer noon, an arm
Rose up from out the bosom of the lake,
Clothed in white samite, mystic, wonderful,
Holding the sword-and how I row'd across
And took it, and have worn it, like a king:
And, wheresoever I am sung or told
In aftertime, this also shall be known:

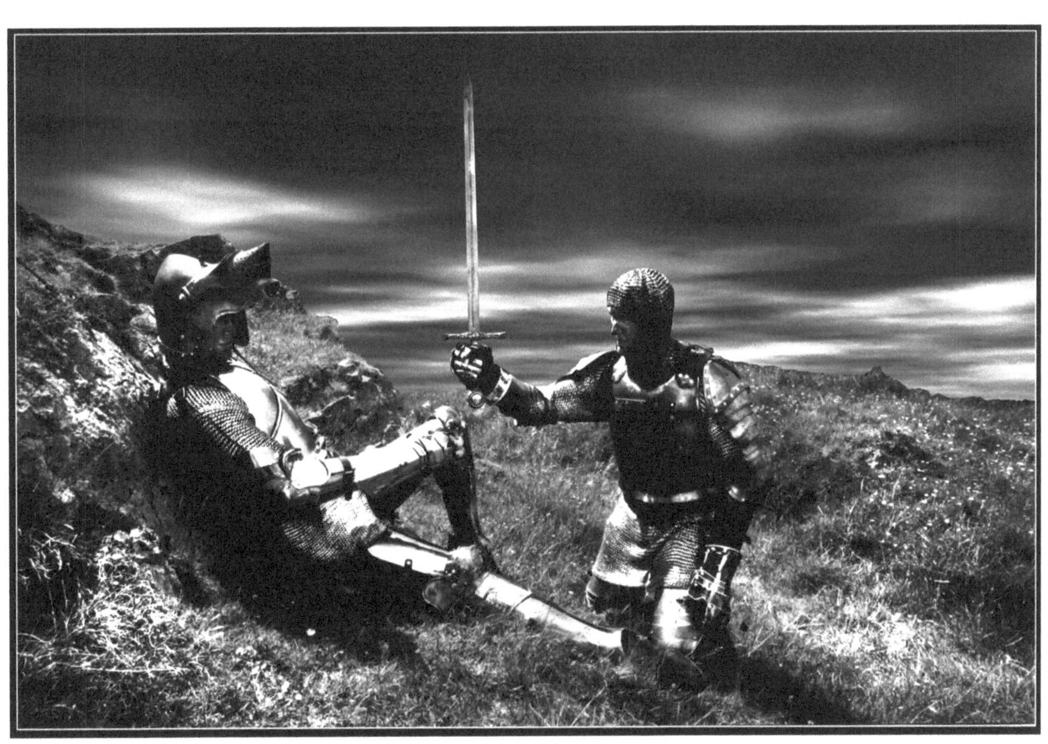

'But now delay not: take Excalibur,
And fling him far into the middle mere:
Watch what thou seëst, and lightly bring me word.'

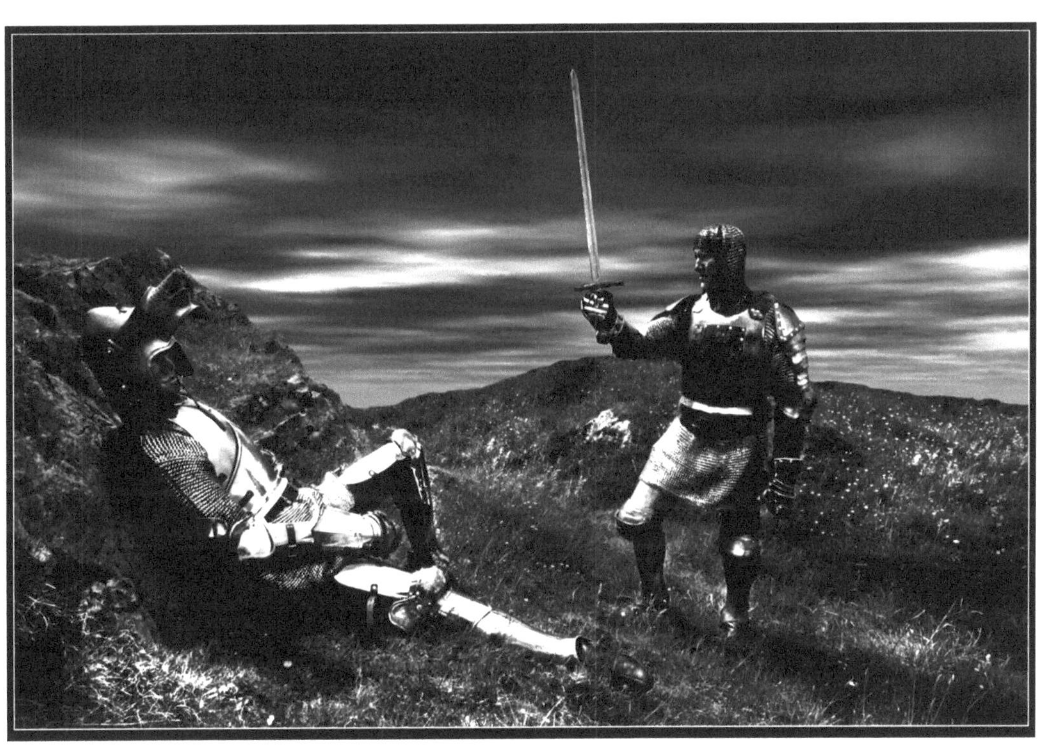

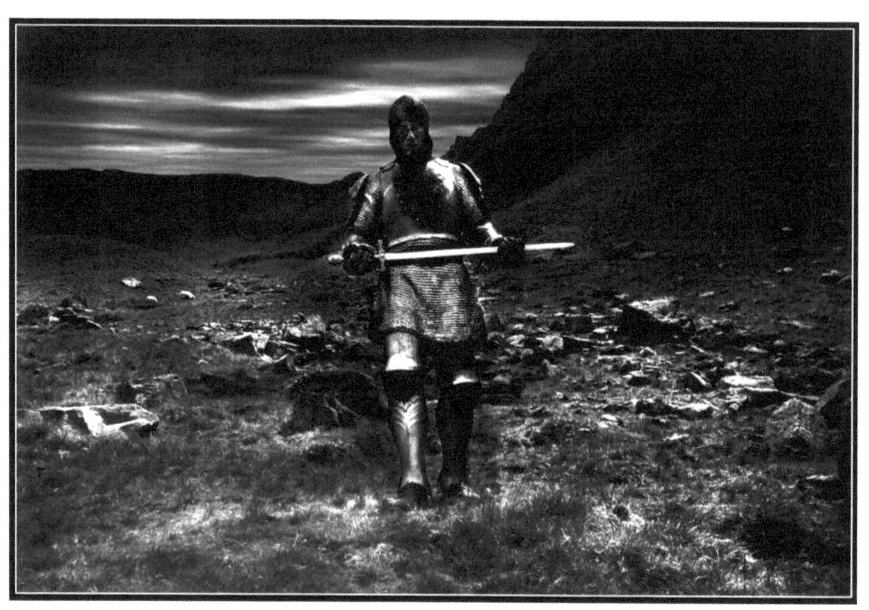

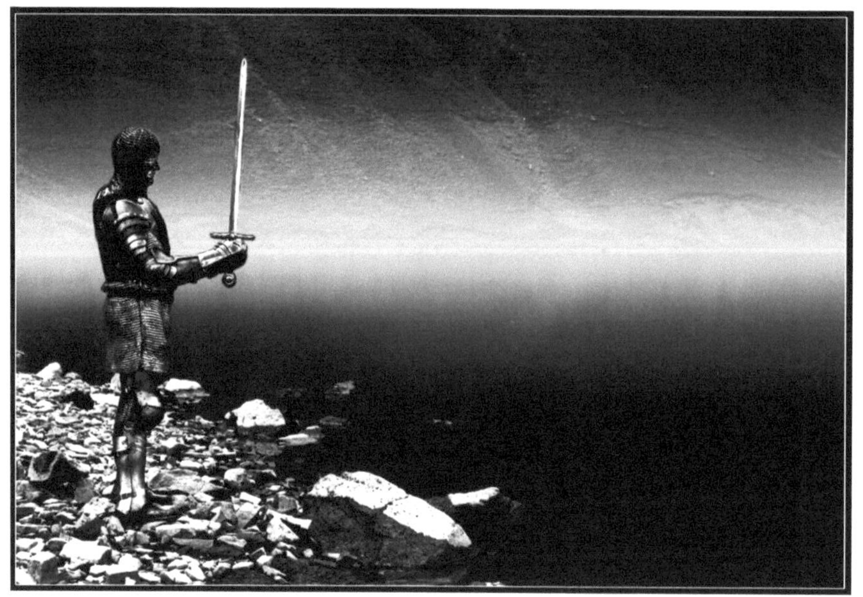

So saying, from the ruin'd shrine he stept
And in the moon athwart the place of tombs,
Where lay the mighty bones of ancient men,
Old knights, and over them the sea-wind sang
Shrill, chill, with flakes of foam. He, stepping down
By zig-zag paths, and juts of pointed rock,
Came on the shining levels of the lake.

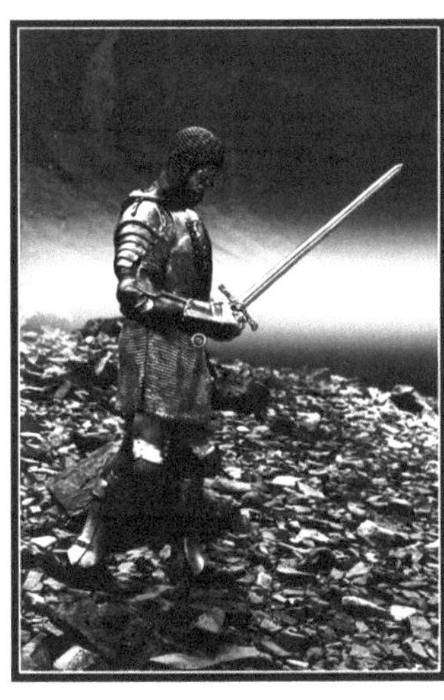

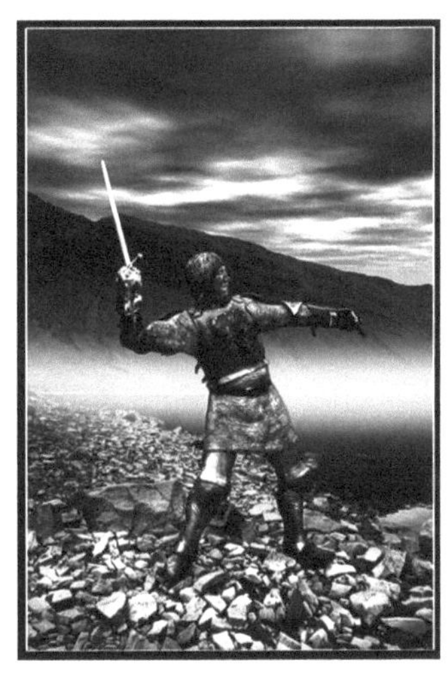

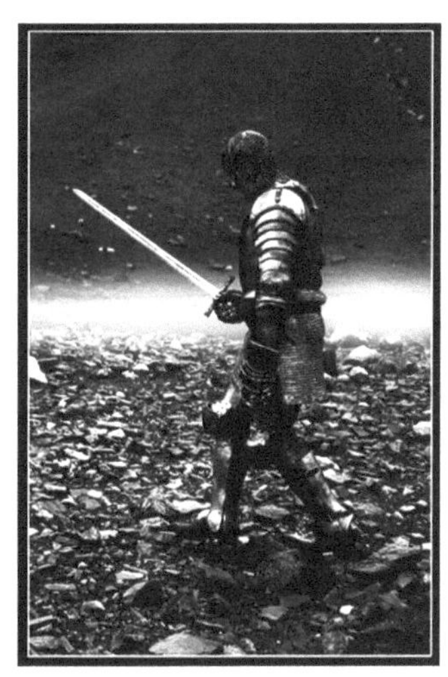

There drew he forth the brand Excalibur,
And o'er him, drawing it, the winter moon,
Brightening the skirts of a long cloud, ran forth
And sparkled keen with frost against the hilt:
For all the haft twinkled with diamond sparks,
Myriads of topaz-lights, and jacinth-work
Of subtlest jewellery. He gazed so long
That both his eyes were dazzled, as he stood,
This way and that dividing the swift mind,
In act to throw: but at last it seem'd
Better to leave Excalibur conceal'd
There in the many-knotted waterflags,
That whistled stiff and dry about the marge.
So strode he back slow to the wounded King.

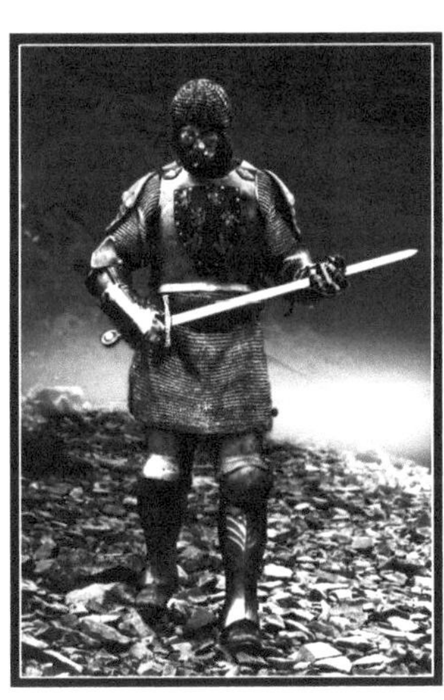

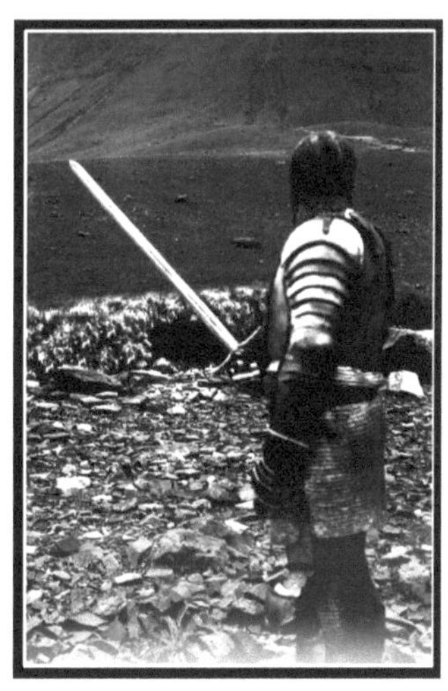

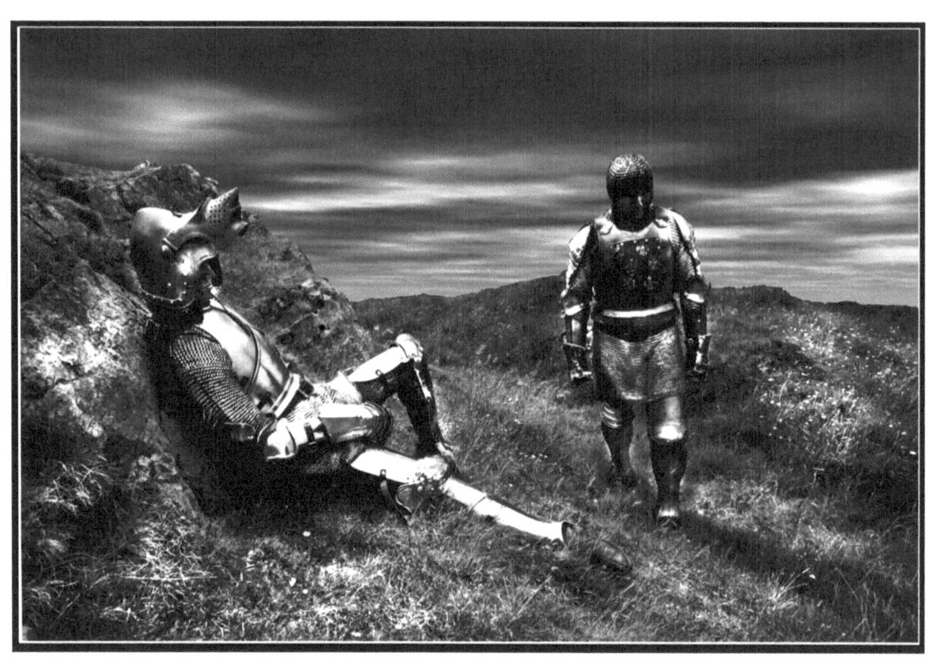

Then spake King Arthur to Sir Bedivere:
'Hast thou perform'd my mission which I gave?
What is it thou hast seen? or what hast heard?'
And answer made the bold Sir Bedivere:
'I heard the ripple washing in the reeds,
And the wild water lapping on the crag.'

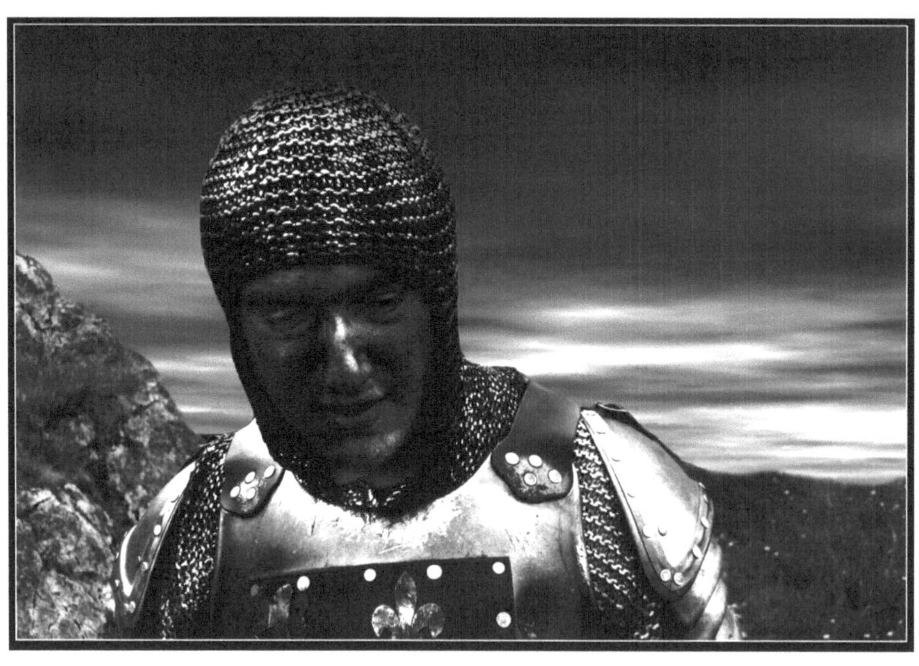

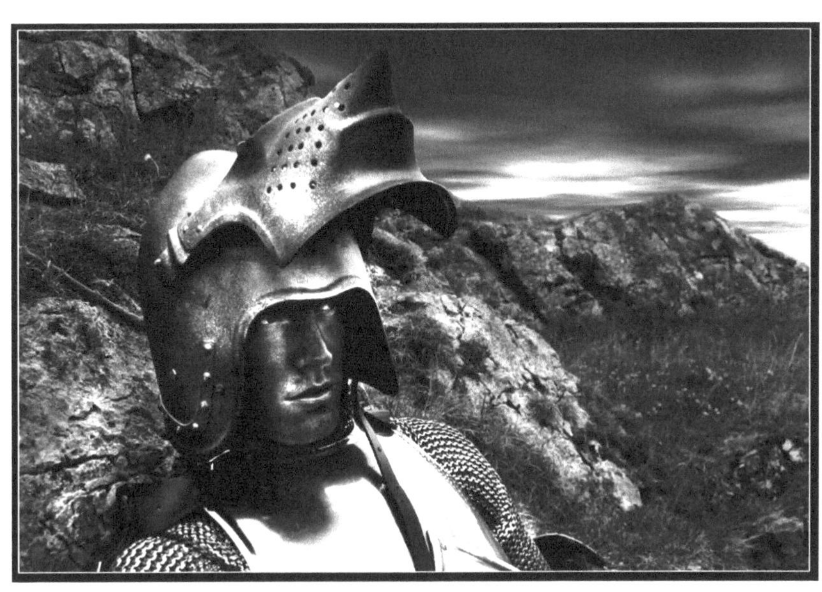

To whom replied King Arthur, faint and pale:
'Thou hast betray'd thy nature and thy name,
Not rendering true answer, as beseem'd
Thy fëalty, nor like a noble knight:
For surer sign had follow'd, either hand,
Or voice, or else a motion of the mere.
This is a shameful thing for men to lie.
Yet now, I charge thee, quickly go again
As thou art lief and dear, and do the thing
I bad thee, watch, and lightly bring me word.'

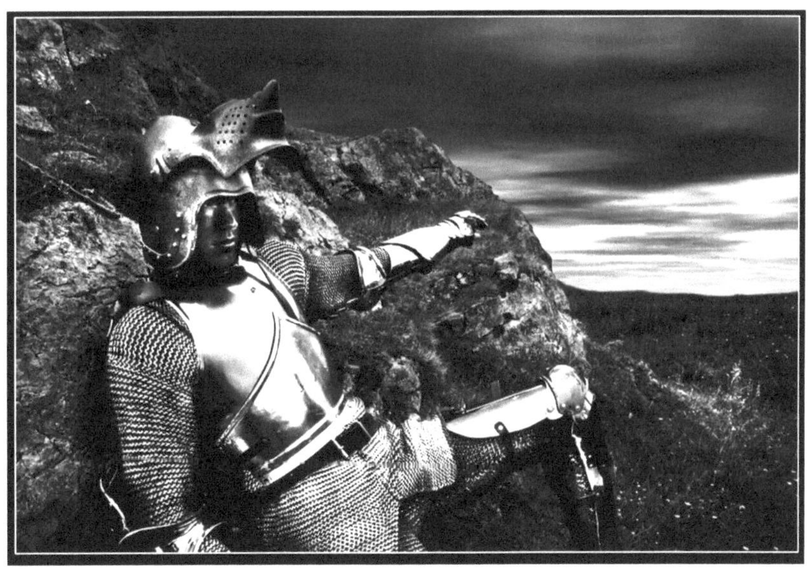

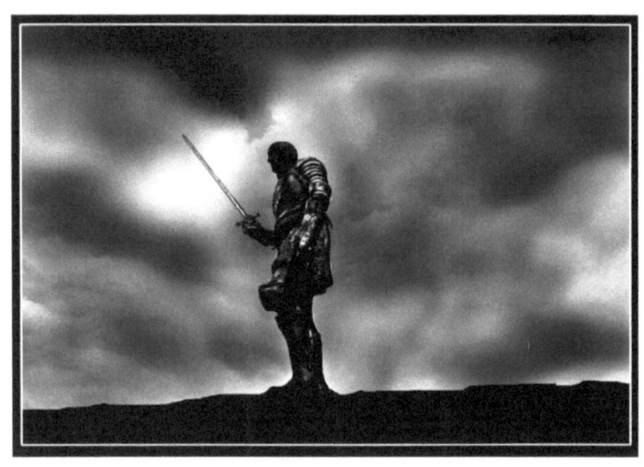

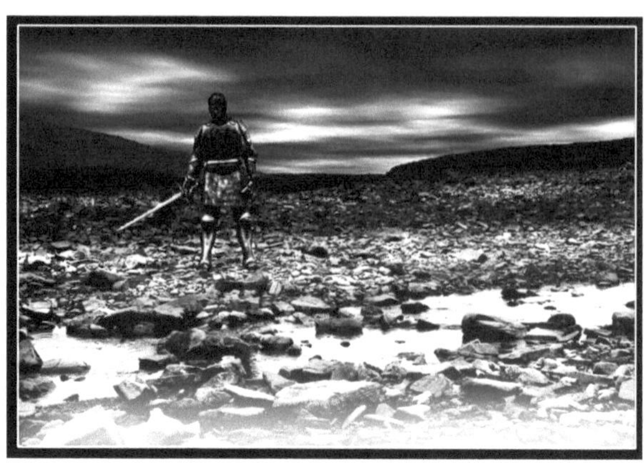

Then went Sir Bedivere the second time
Across the ridge, and paced beside the mere,
Counting the dewy pebbles, fix'd in thought;
But when he saw the wonder of the hilt,
How curiously and strangely chased, he smote
His palms together, and he cride out aloud,
'And if indeed I cast the brand away,
Surely a precious thing, one worthy note,
Should thus be lost for ever from the earth,
Which might have pleased the eyes of many men.'

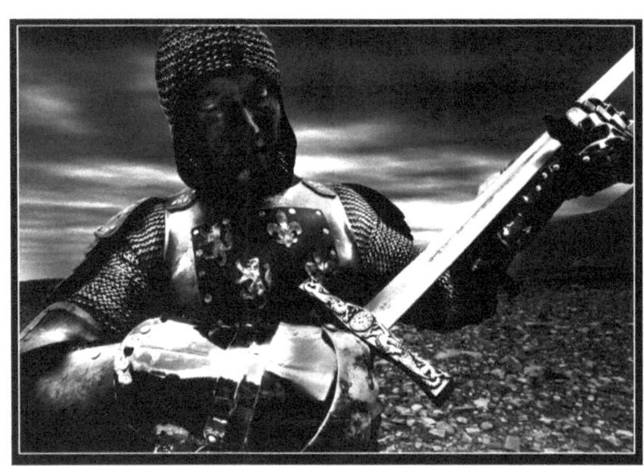

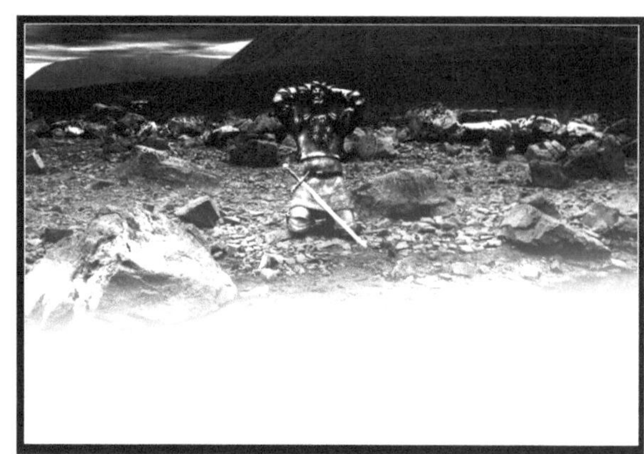

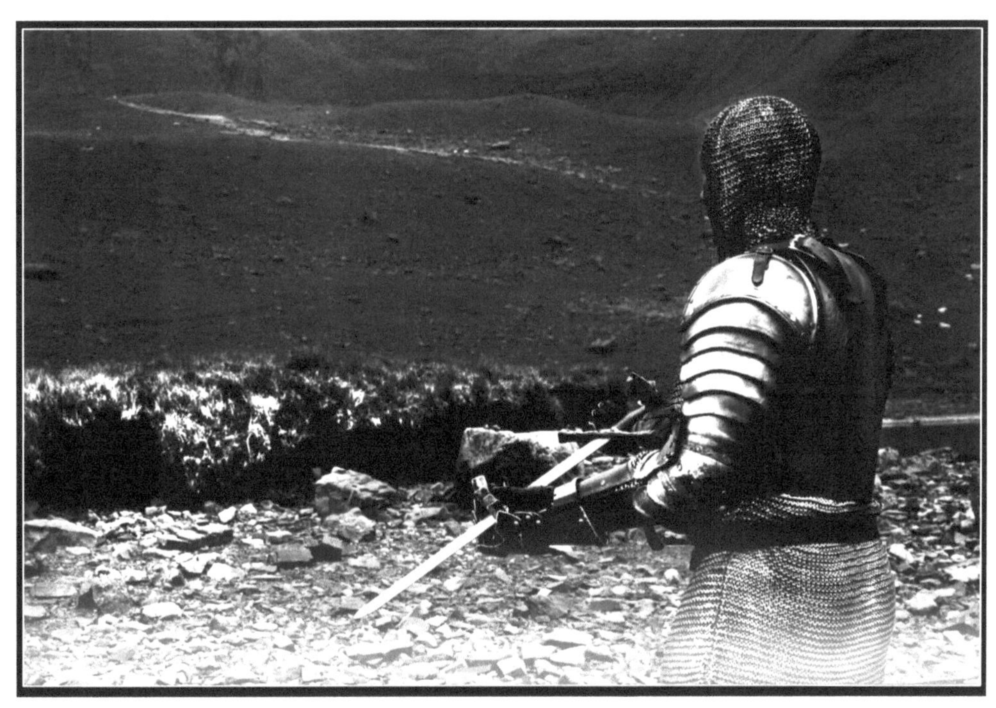

So spake he, clouded with his own conceit,
And hid Excalibur the second time,
And strode back slow to the wounded King.

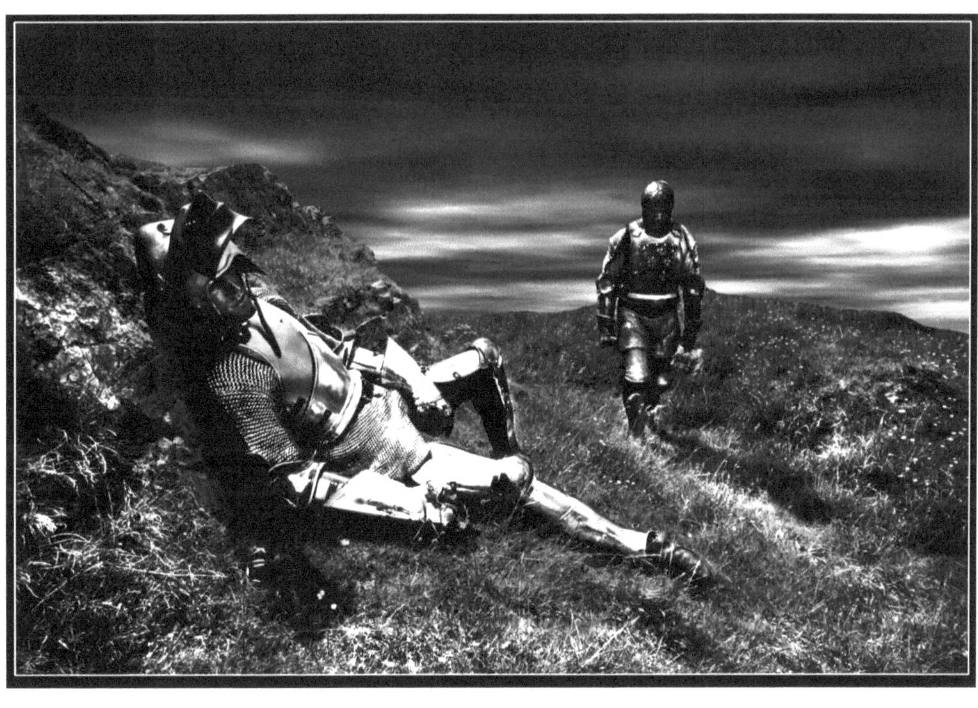

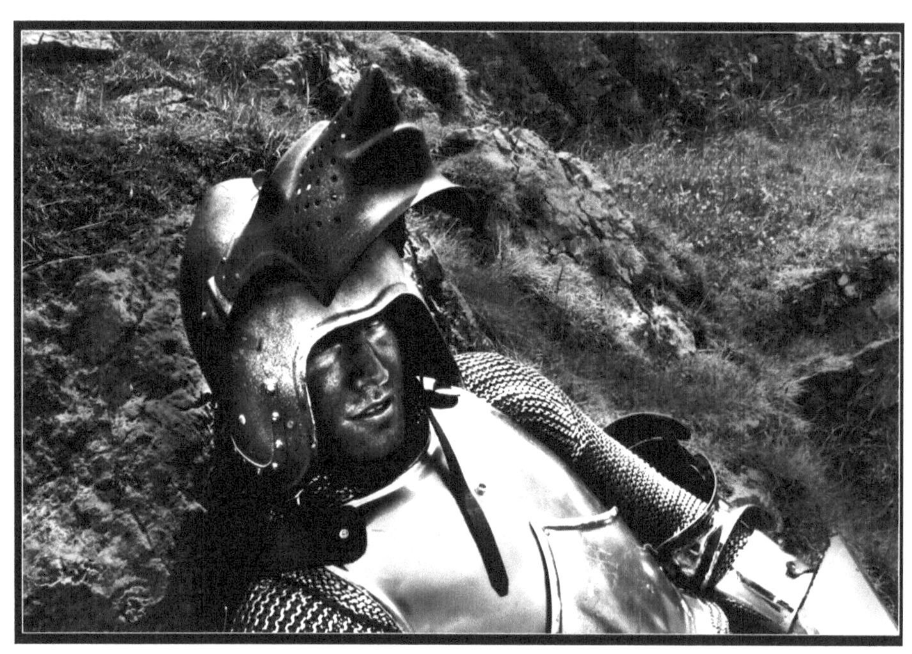

Then spoke King Arthur, breathing heavily:
'What is it thou hast seen? or what hast heard?'
And answer made the bold Sir Bedivere:
'I heard the water lapping on the crag,
And the long ripple washing in the reeds.'

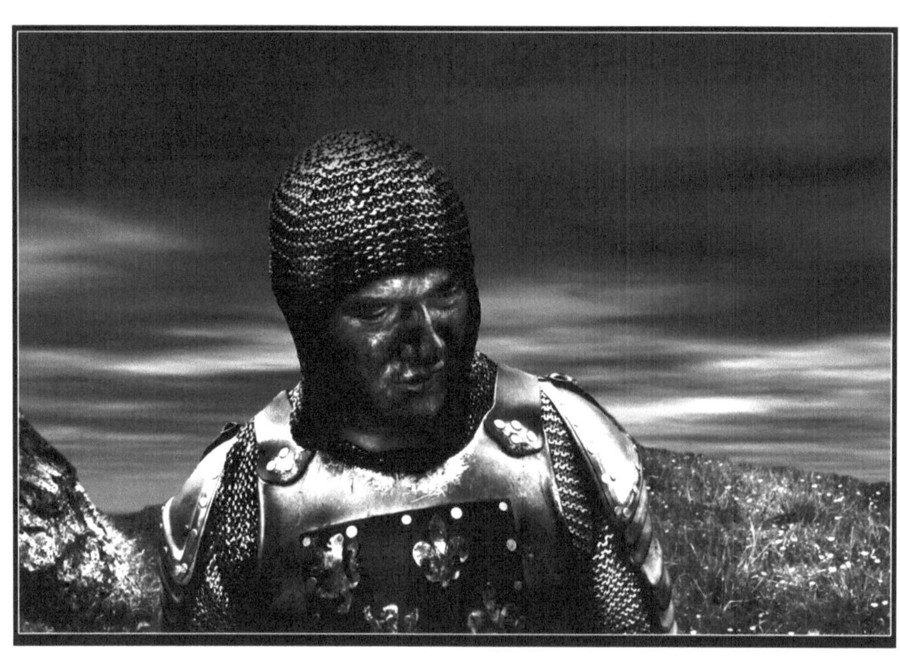

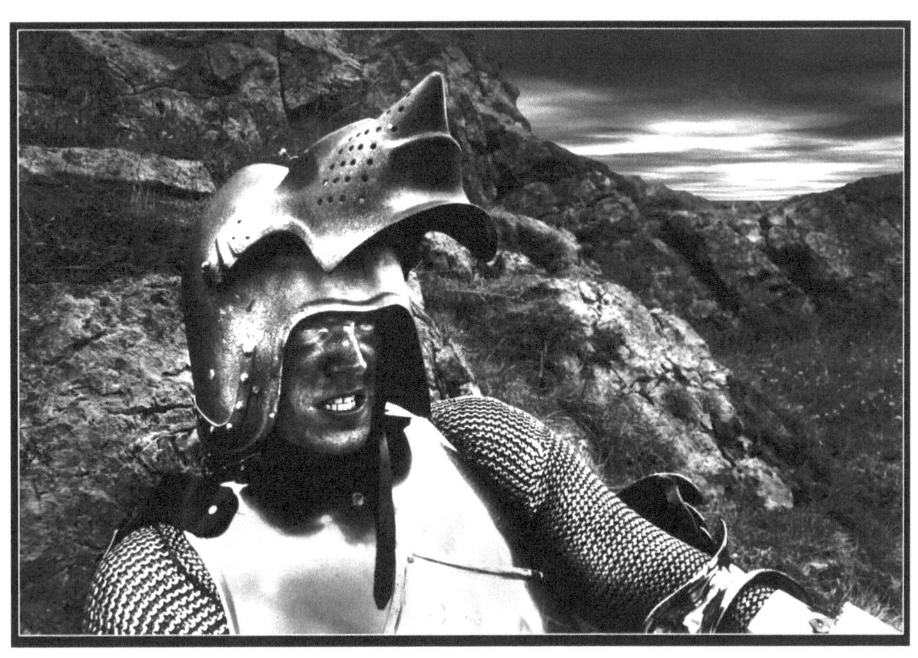

To whom replied King Arthur, much in wrath:
'Ah, miserable and unkind, untrue,
Unknightly, traitor-hearted! Woe is me!
Authority forgets a dying king,
Yet, for a man to fail in duty twice,
And the third time may prosper, get thee hence:
But, if thou spare to fling Excalibur,
I will arise and slay thee with my hands.'

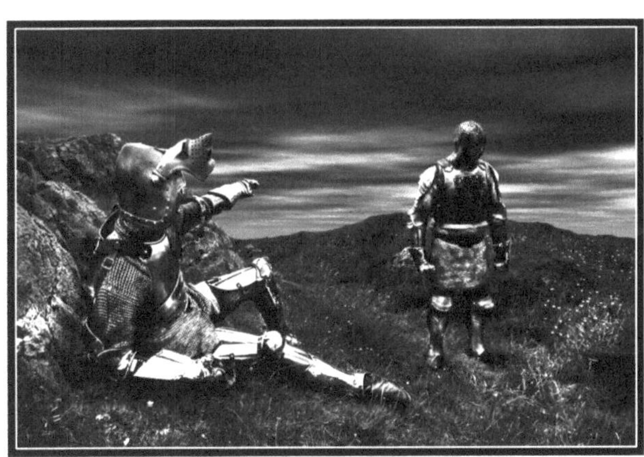

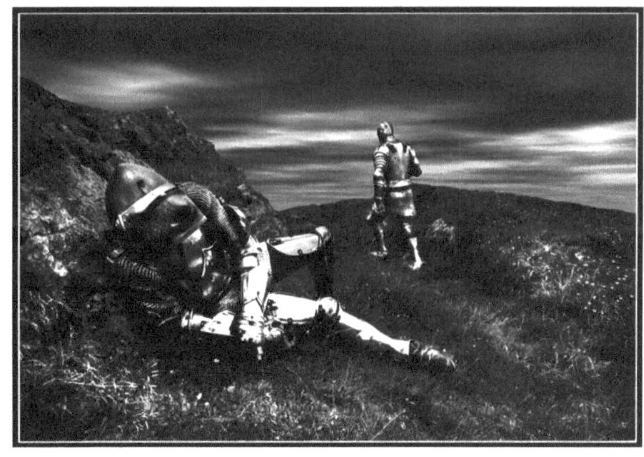

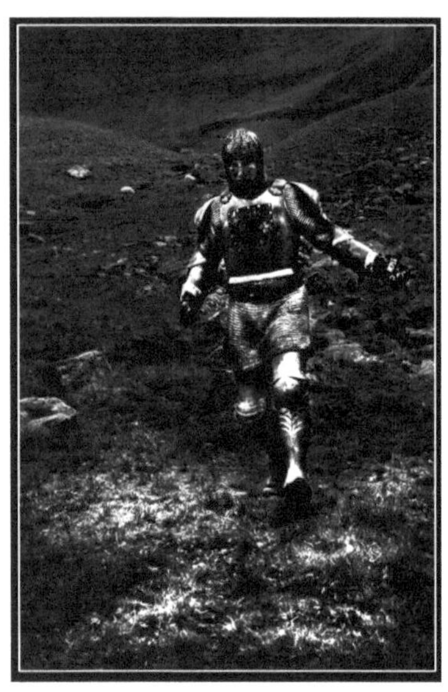

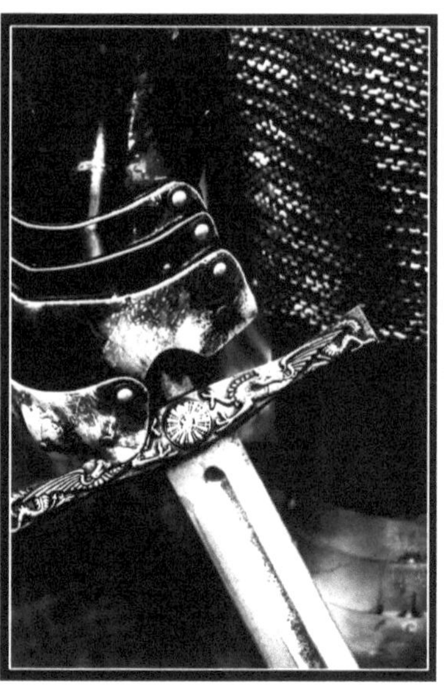

Then quickly rose Sir Bedivere, and ran,
And, leaping down the ridges lightly, plunged
Among the bulrush-beds, and clutch'd the sword,
And strongly wheel'd and threw it.

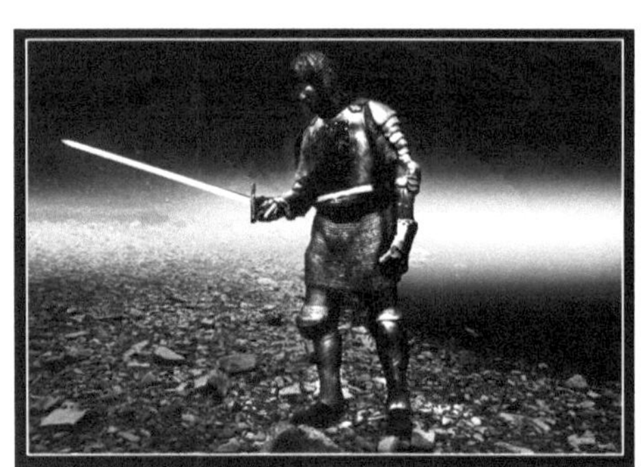

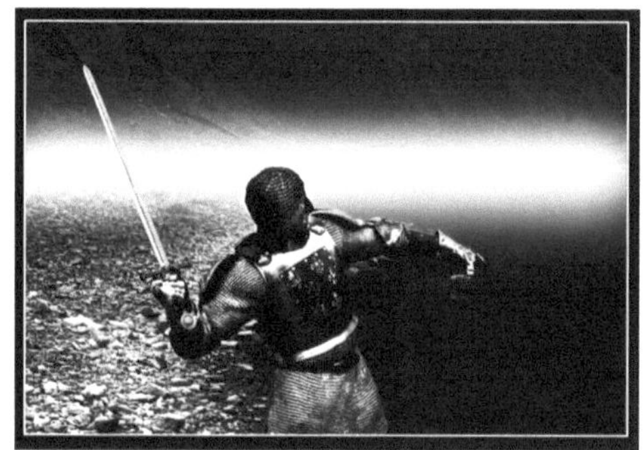

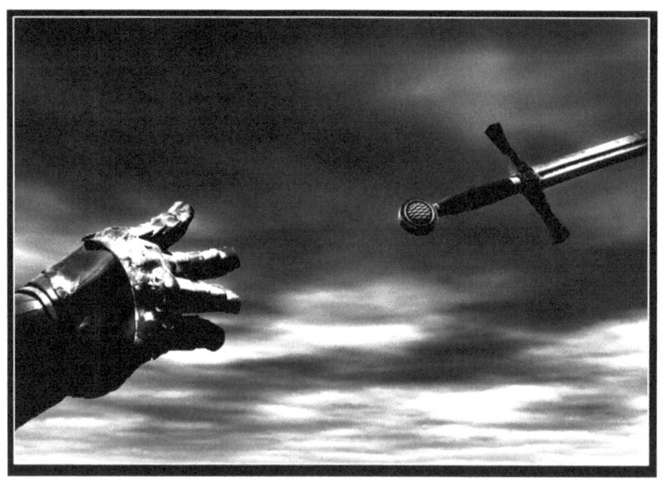

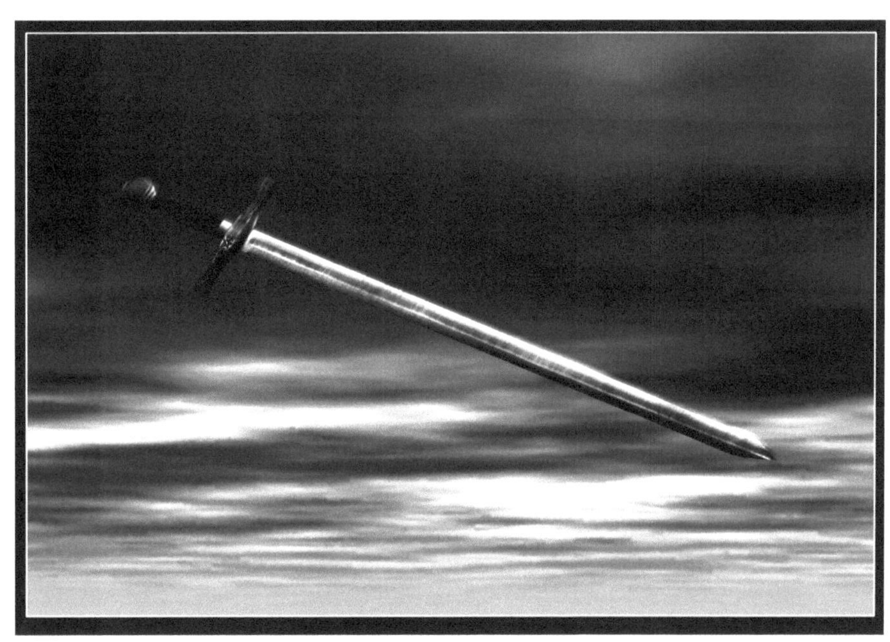

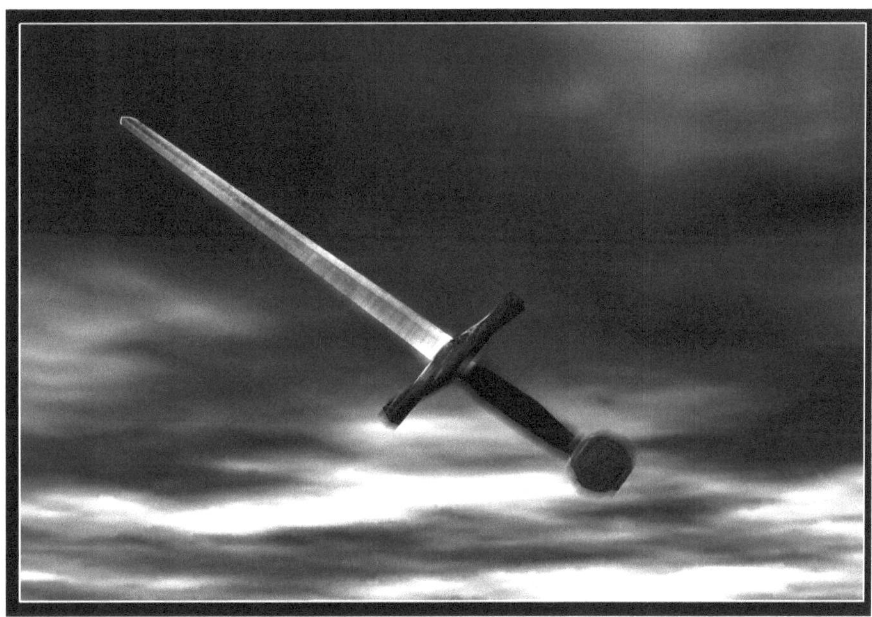

The great brand made lightnings in the splendour of the moon,
And flashing round and round, and whirl'd in an arch,
Shot like a streamer of the northern morn,
Seen where the moving isles of winter shock by night,
With noises of the northern sea.
So flash'd and fell the brand Excalibur:

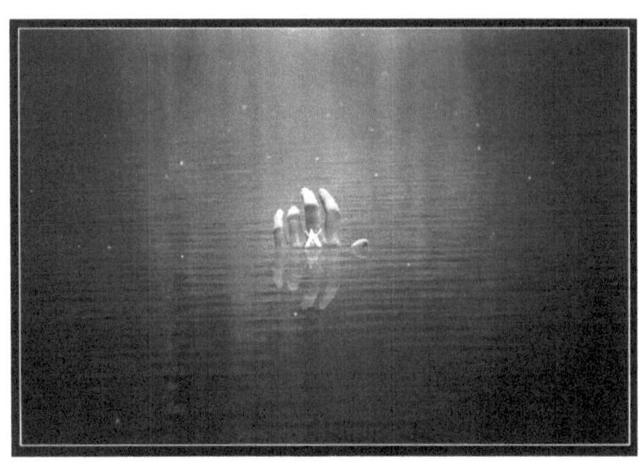

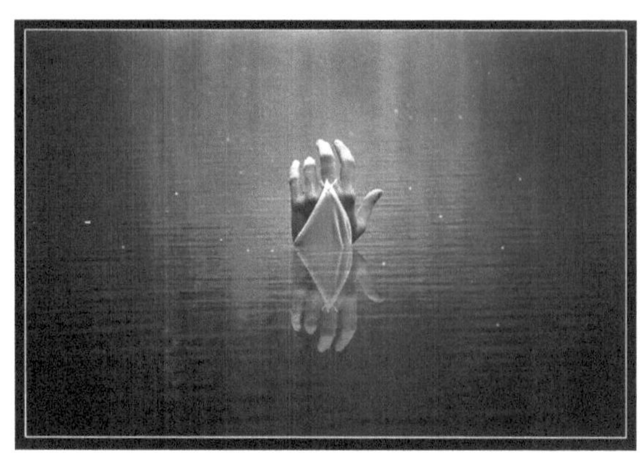

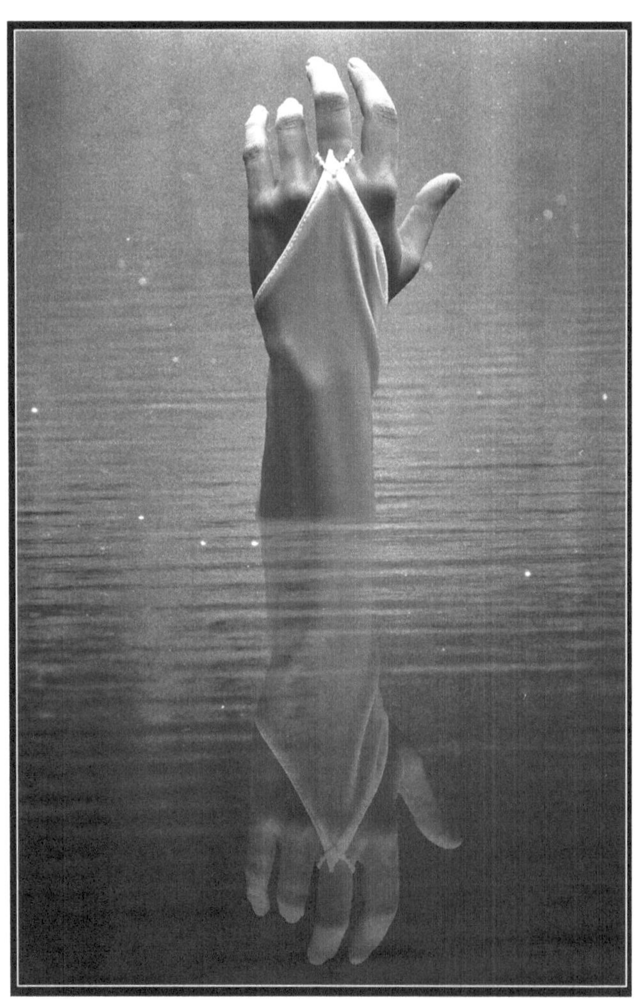

But ere he dipt the surface, rose an arm
Clothed in white samite, mystic, wonderful...

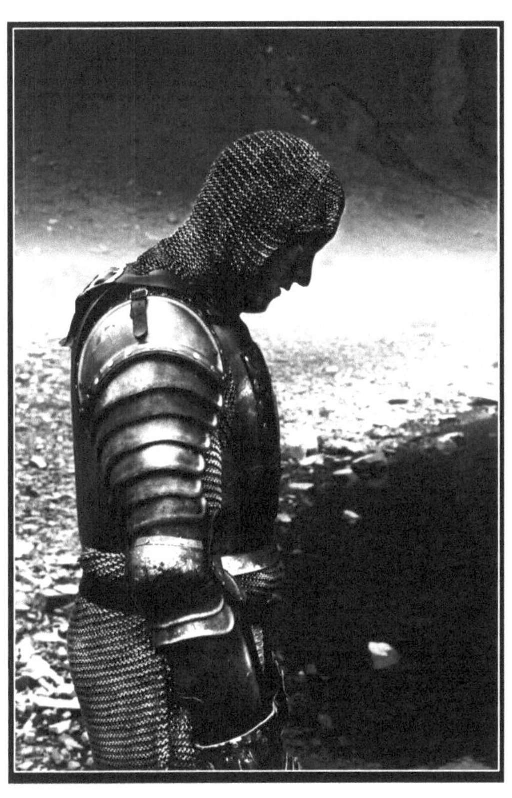
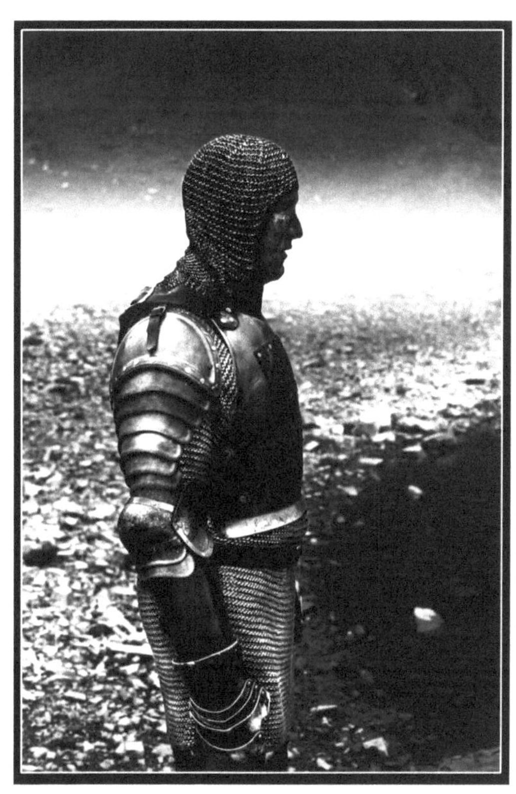
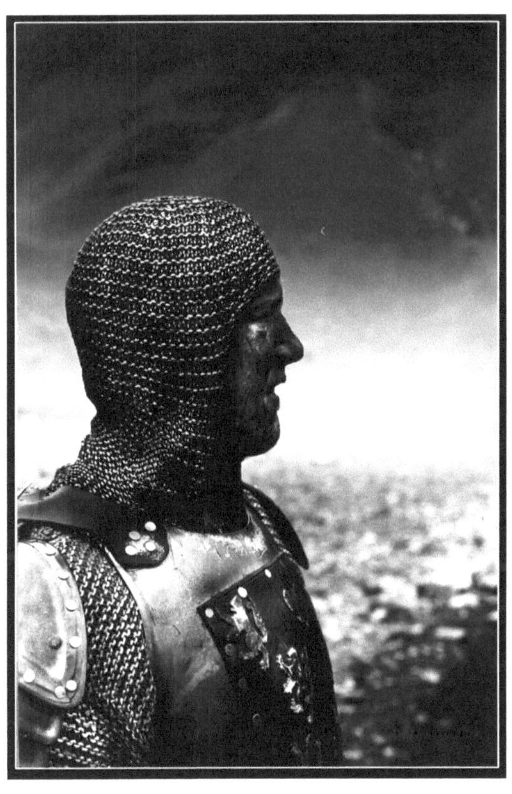
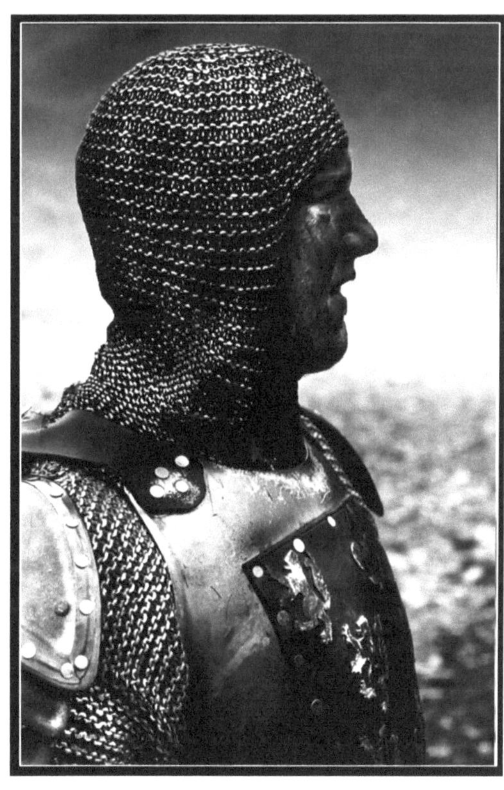

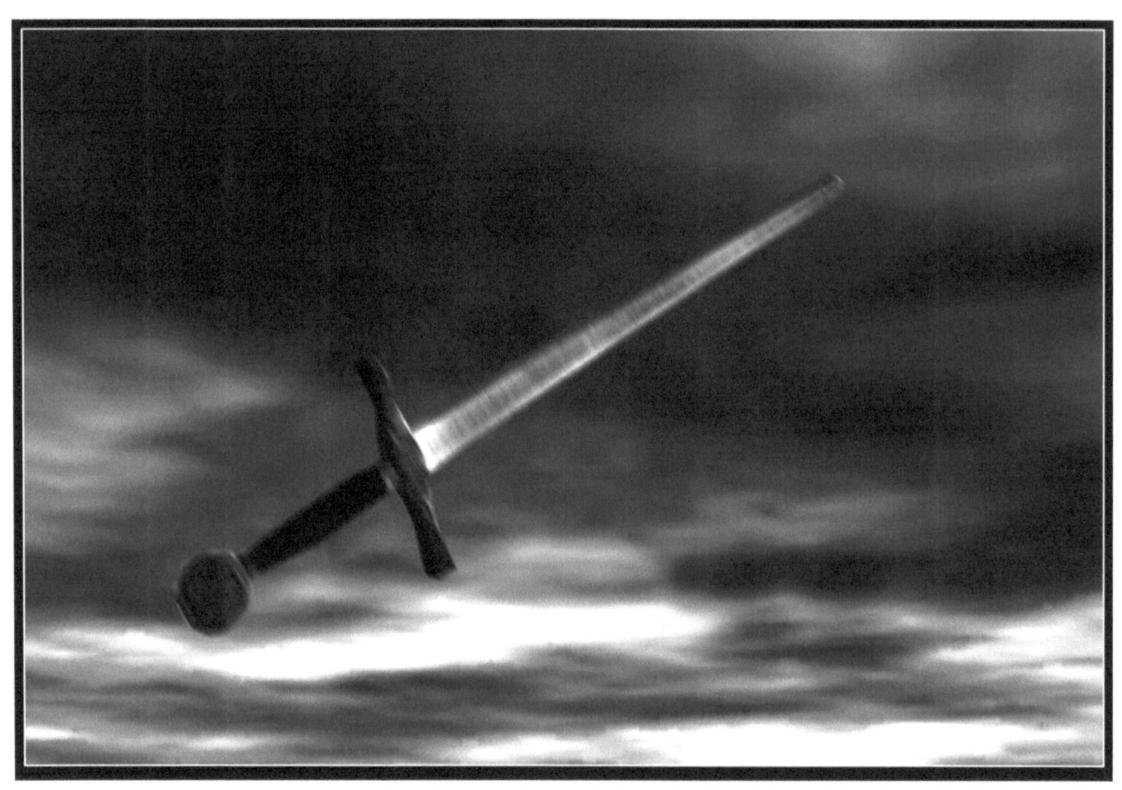

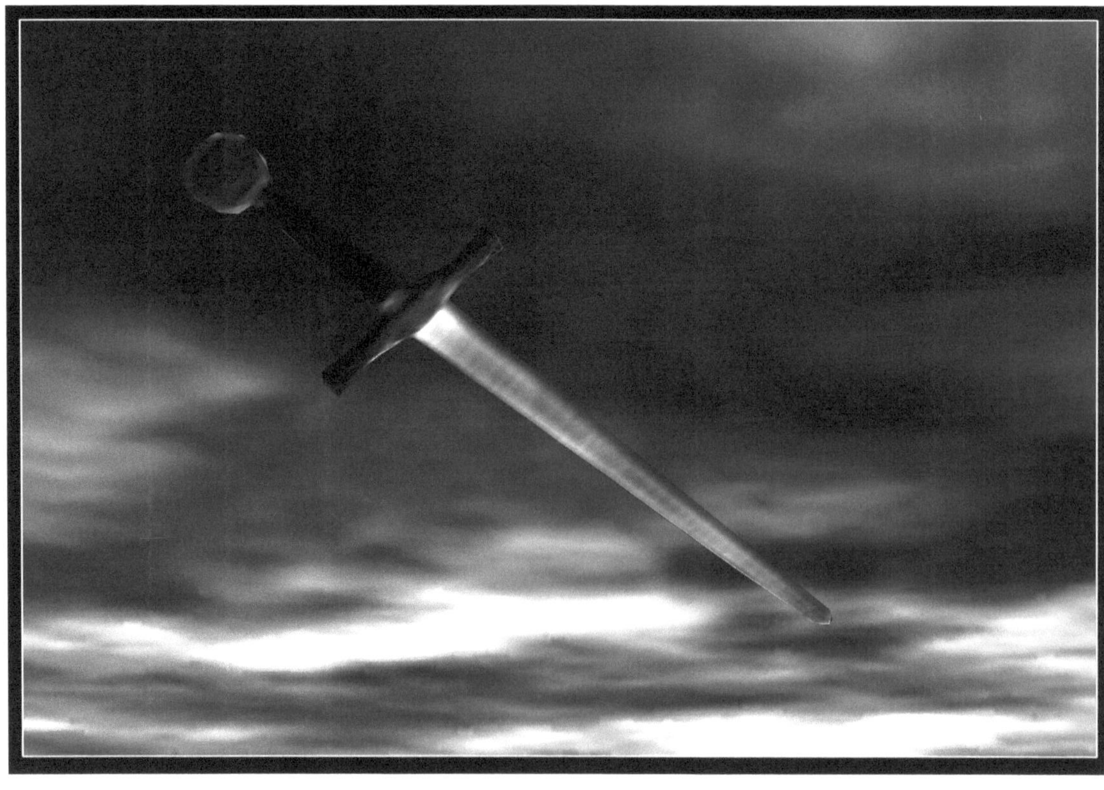

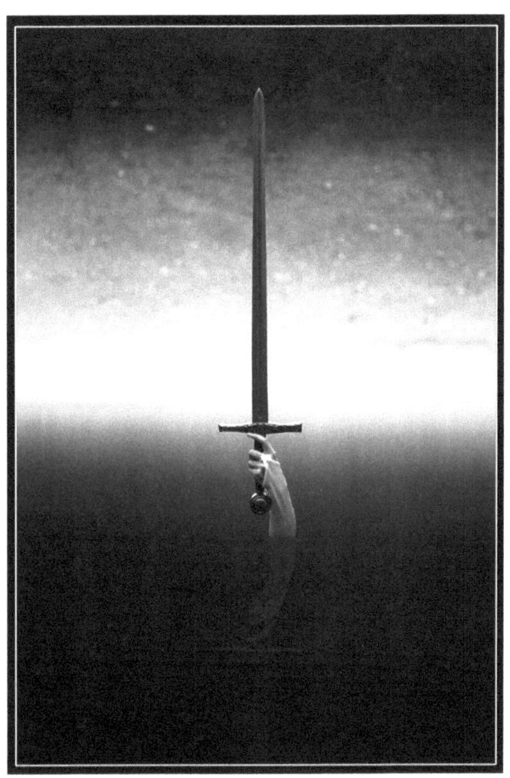

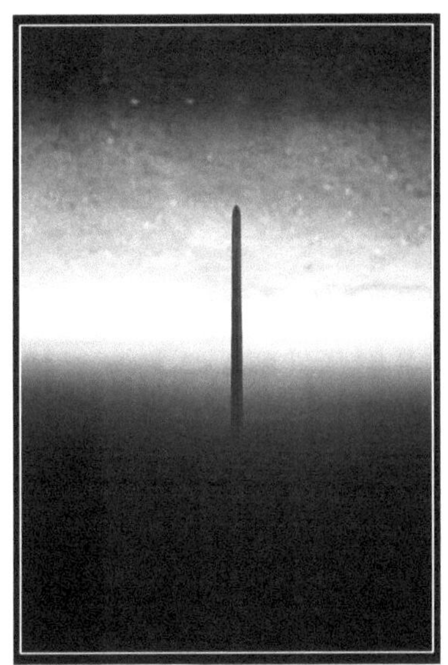

...And caught him by the hilt, and brandish'd him
Three times, and drew him under in the mere.
And lightly went the the other to the King.

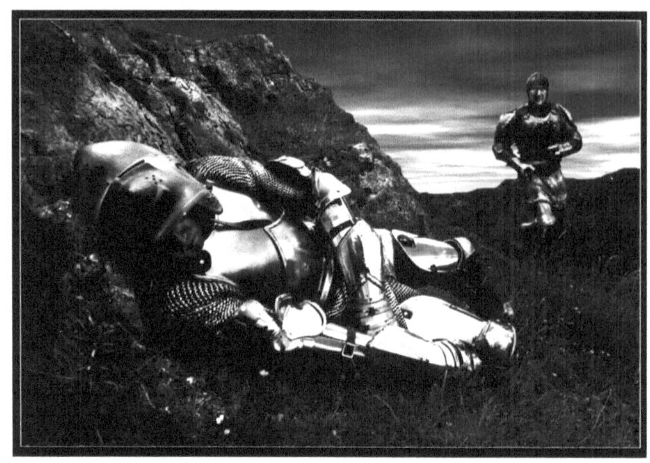

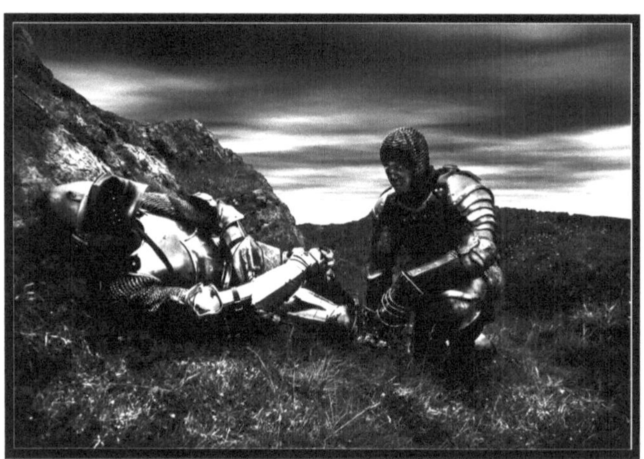

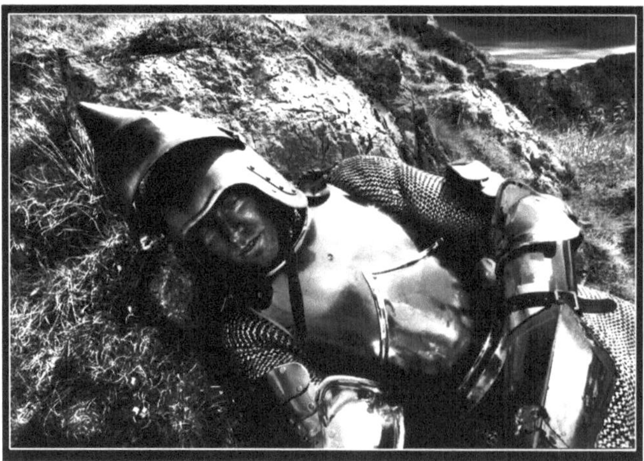

Then spoke King Arthur, drawing thicker breath:
'Now see I by thine eyes that this is done.
Speak out: what is it thou hast heard, or seen?'

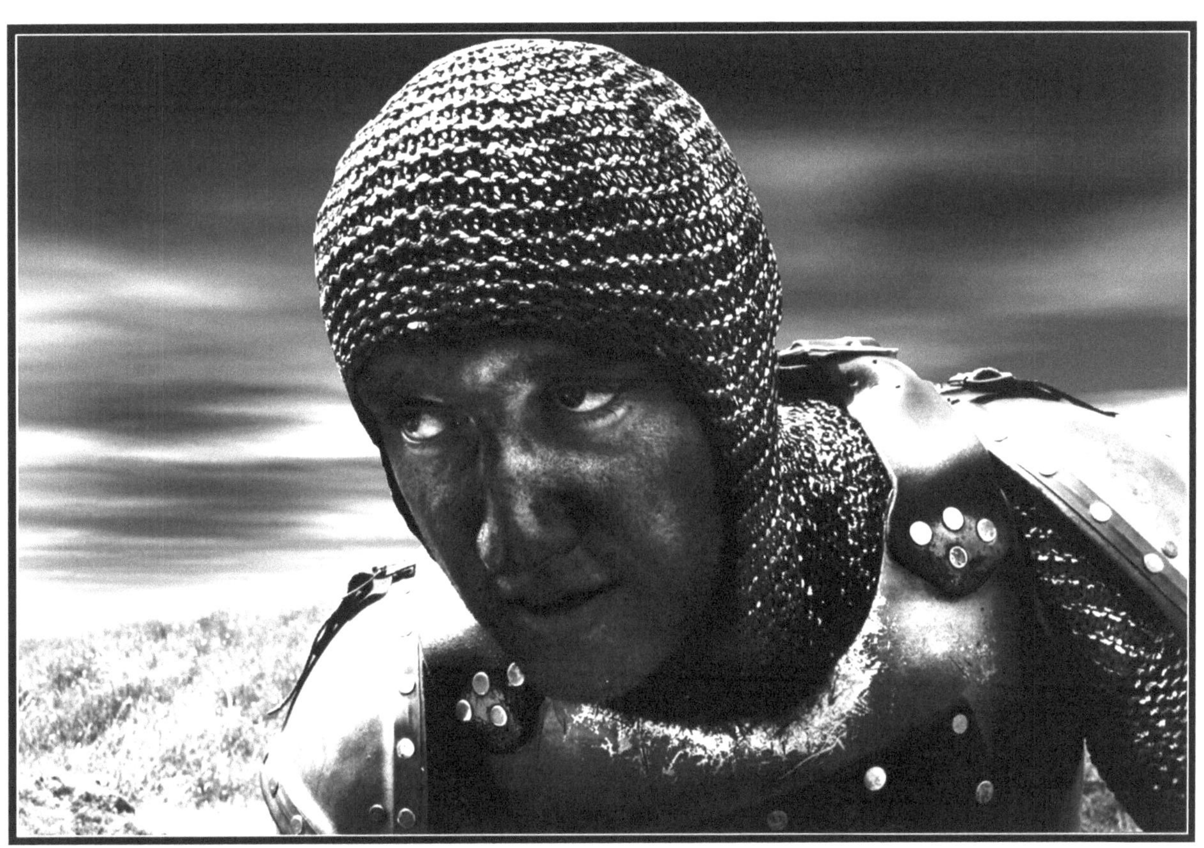

And answer made the bold Sir Bedivere:
'Sir King, I closed mine eyelids, lest the gems
Should blind my purpose, for I never saw,
Nor shall I see, here or elsewhere, till I die,
Not tho' I live three lives of mortal men,
So great a miracle as yonder hilt.
The, with both hands I flung him, wheeling him;
But when I look'd again, behold an arm,
Clothed in white samite, mystic, wonderful,
That caught him by the hilt, and brandish'd him
Three times and drew him under in the mere.'

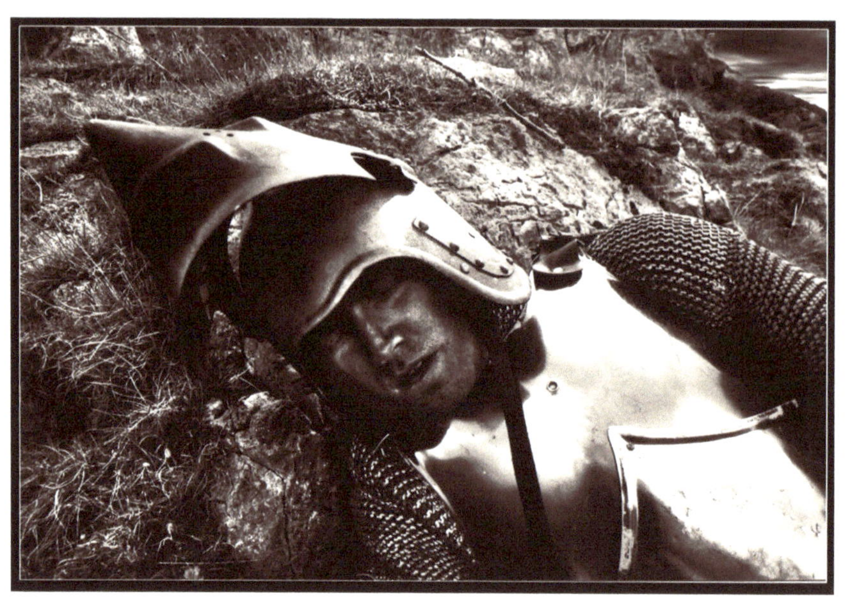

And answer made King Arthur, breathing hard:
'My end draws nigh; 'tis time that I were gone.
Make broad thy shoulders to recieve my weight,
And bear me to the margin; yet I fear
My wound hath taken cold, and I shall die.'

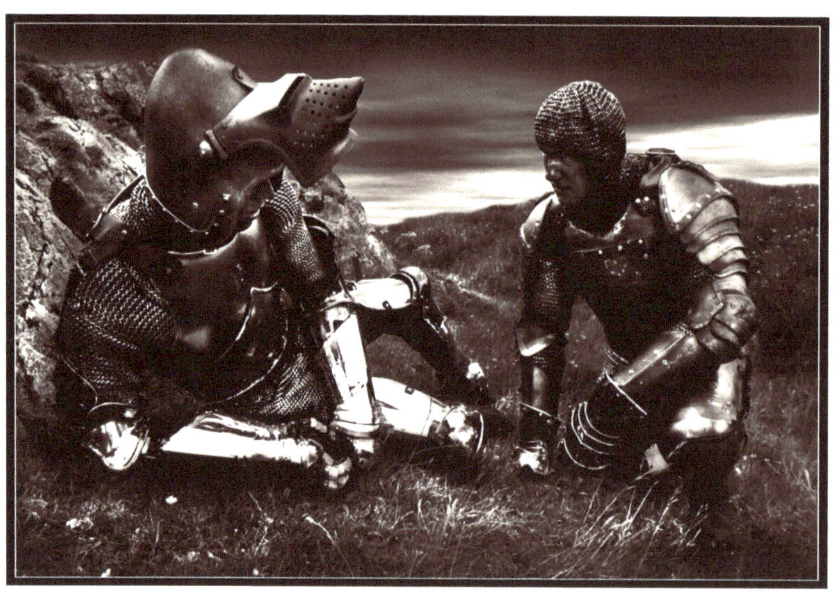

So saying, from the pavement he half rose,
Slowly, with pain, reclining on his arm.

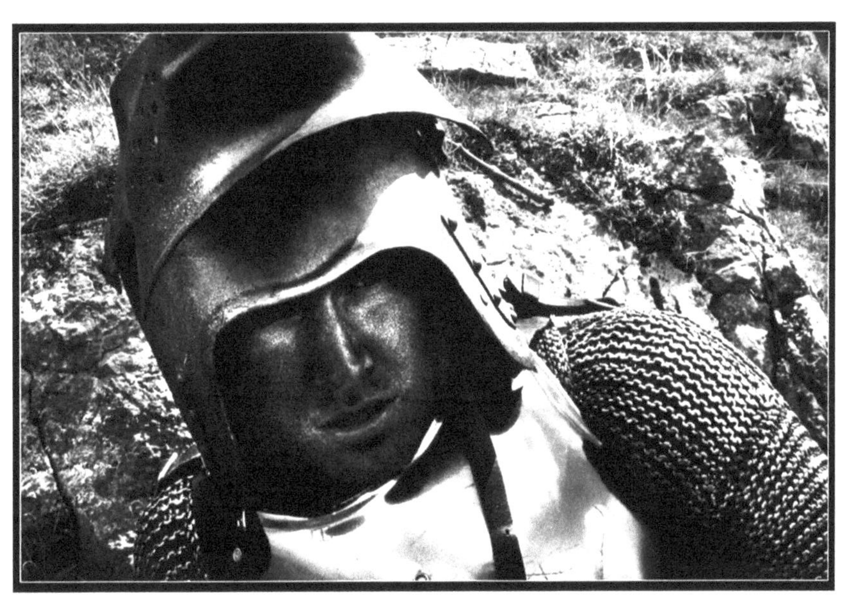

And looking wistfully with wide blue eyes,
As in a picture.

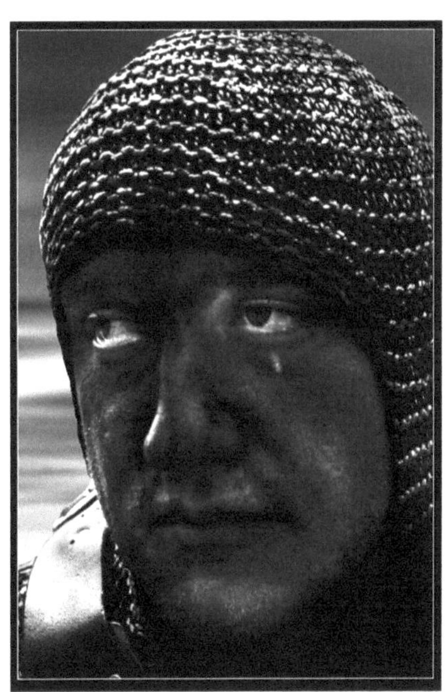

Him Sir Bedivere
Remorsefully regarded thro' his tears,
And would have spoken, but he found not words...

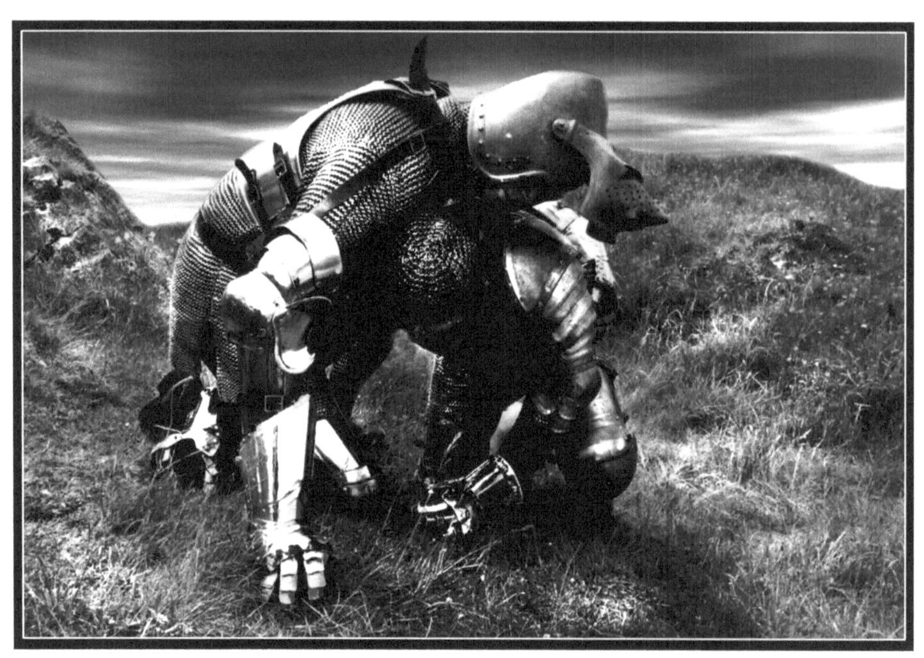

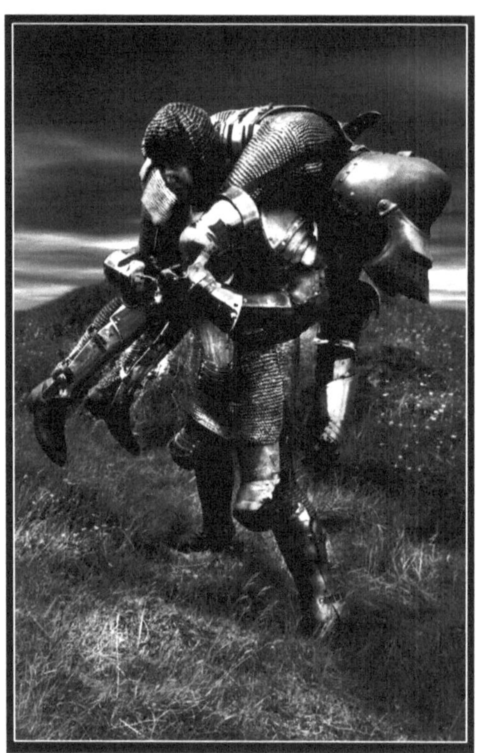

...Then took with care, and kneeling on one knee,
o'er both his shoulders drew the languid hands,
And rising bore him thro' the place of tombs.

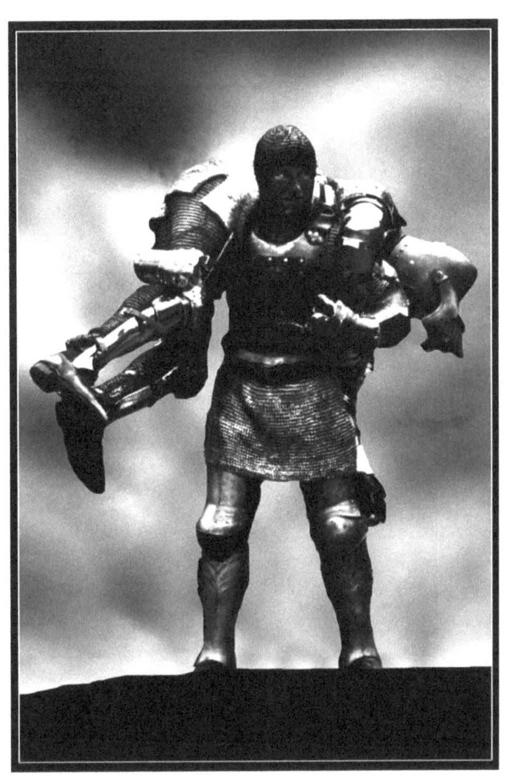

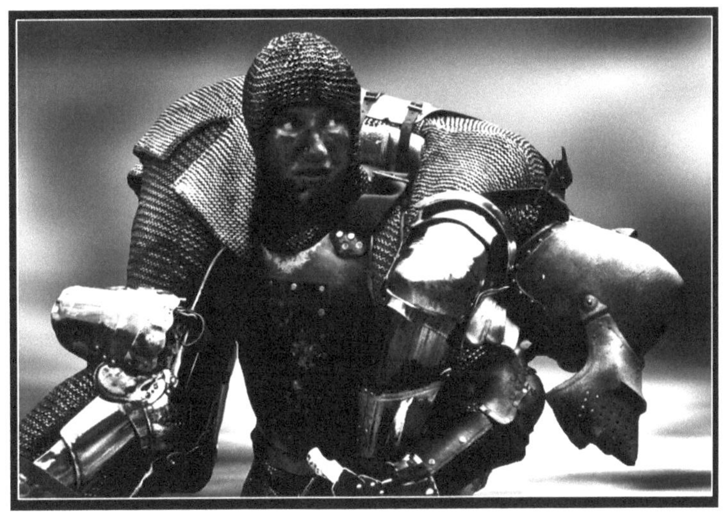

But, as he walk'd, King Arthur panted hard,
Like one that feels a nightmare on his bed
When all the house is mute. So sigh'd the King,
Muttering and murmering at his ear, 'Quick, quick!
I fear it is too late, and I shall die.'

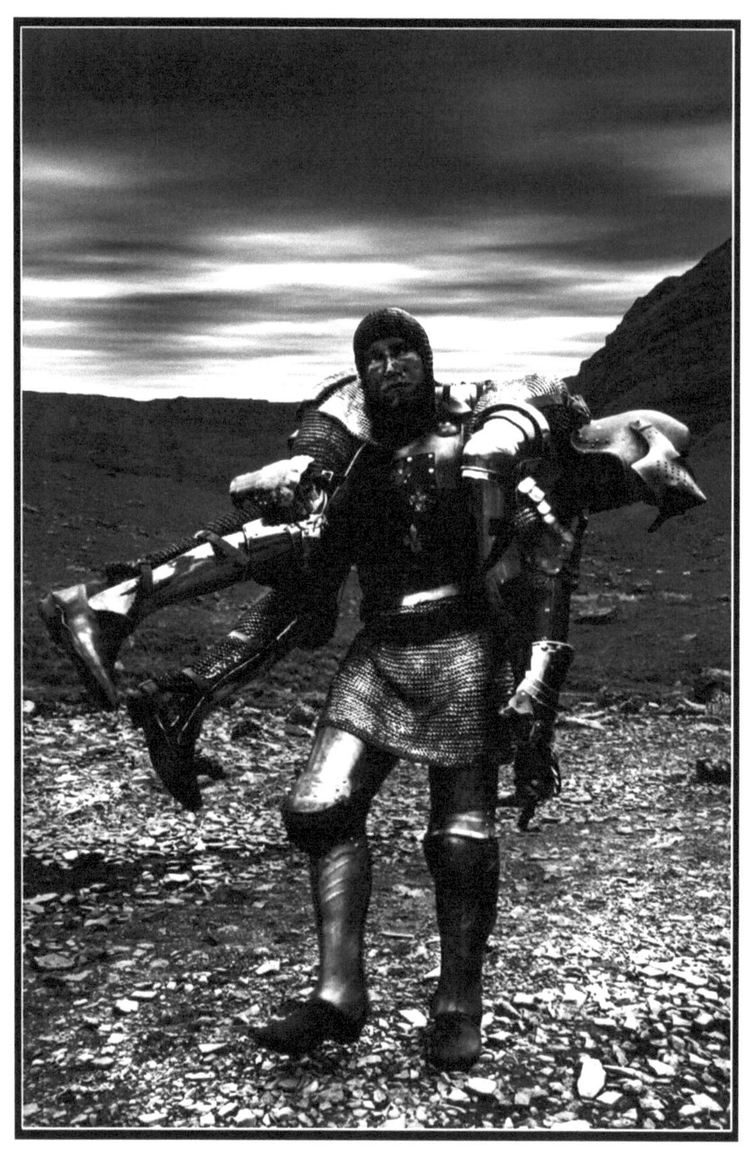

But the other swiftly strode from ridge to ridge,
Clothed with his breath, and looking, as he walk'd,
Larger than human on the frozen hills.
He heard the deep behind him, and a cry before.
His own thought drove him, like a goad.
Dry clash'd his harness in the icy caves
And barren chasms, and all to the left and right
The bare black cliff clang'd round him, as he based
His feet on juts of slippery crag that rang
Sharp-smitten with the dint of armed heels-

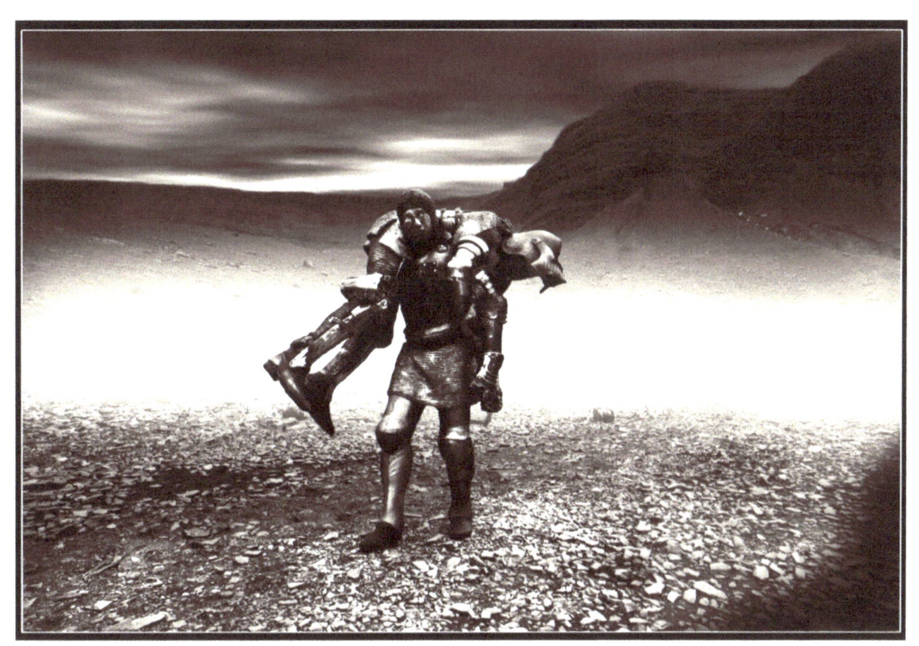

-And on a sudden, lo! the level lake,
And the long glories of the winter moon.

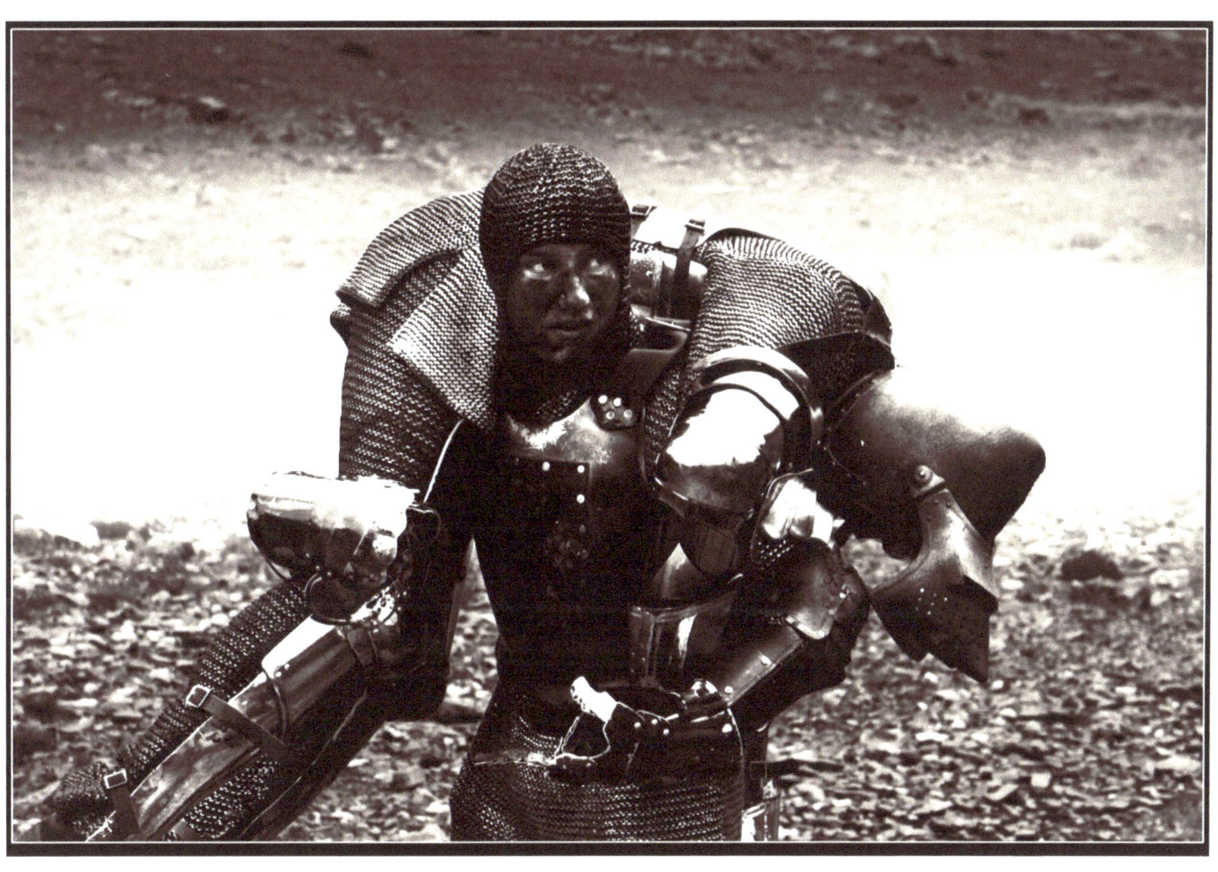

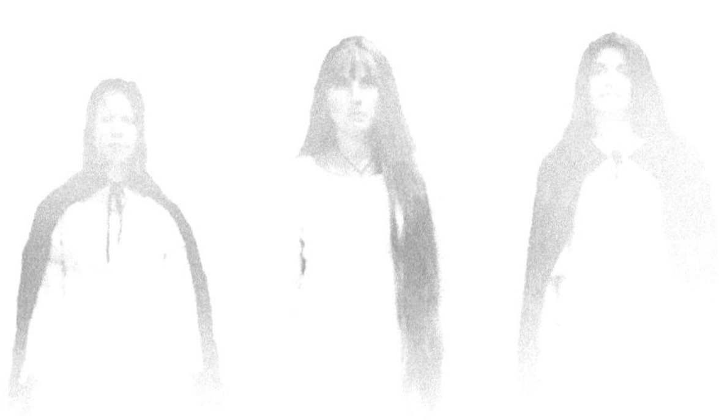

Then saw they how there hove a dusky barge,
Dark as a funeral scarf from stem to stern,
Beneath them; and descending they were ware
That all the decks were dense with stately forms
Black-stoled, black-hooded, like a dream-by these Three Queens

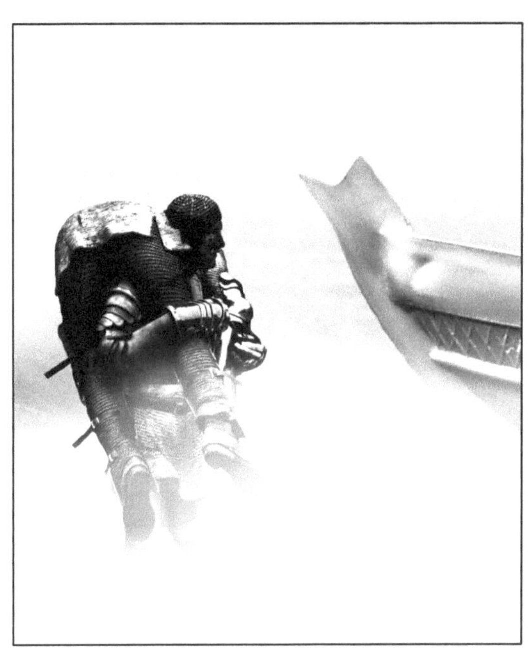

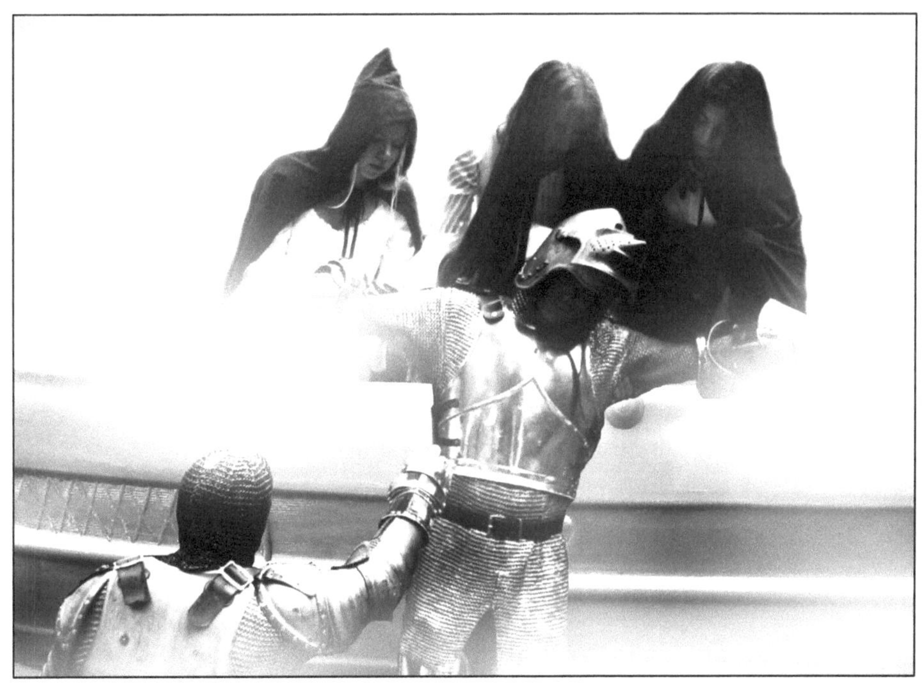

Then murmur'd Arthur, 'Place me in the barge,'
And to the barge they came. There those three Queens
Put forth their hands, and took the King, and wept.

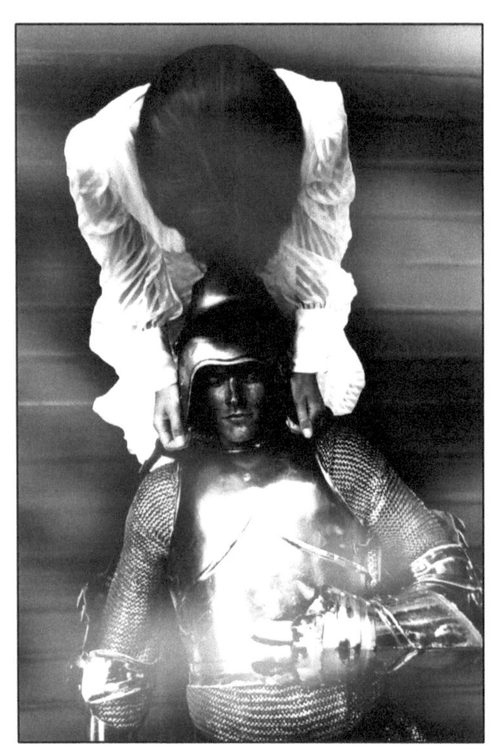

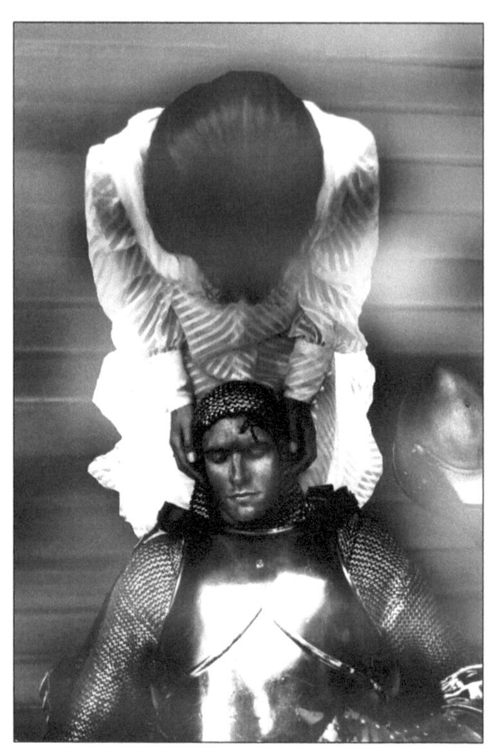

But she, that rose the tallest of them all
And fairest, laid his head upon her lap,
And loosed the shatter'd casque, and chafed his hands,
And call'd him by his name, complaining loud,
And dropping bitter tears against his brow
Striped with dark blood: for all his face was white
And colourless, and like the wither'd moon
Smote by the fresh beam of the springing east.

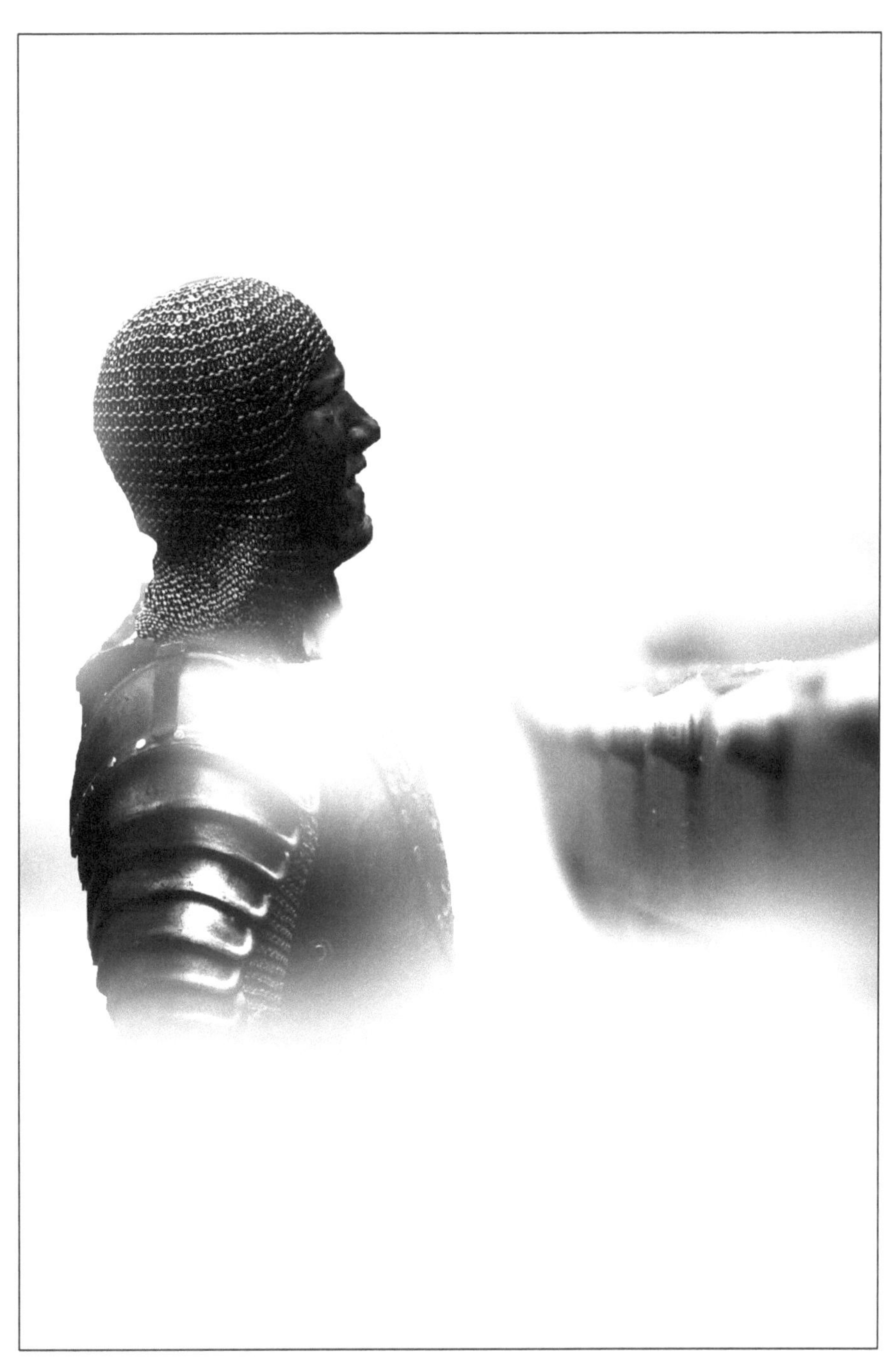

Then loudly cried the bold Sir Bedivere,
'Ah! my Lord Arthur, whither shall I go?
Where shall I hide my forehead and my eyes?
For now I see the true old times are dead,
When every morning brought a noble chance,
And every chance brought out a noble knight.'

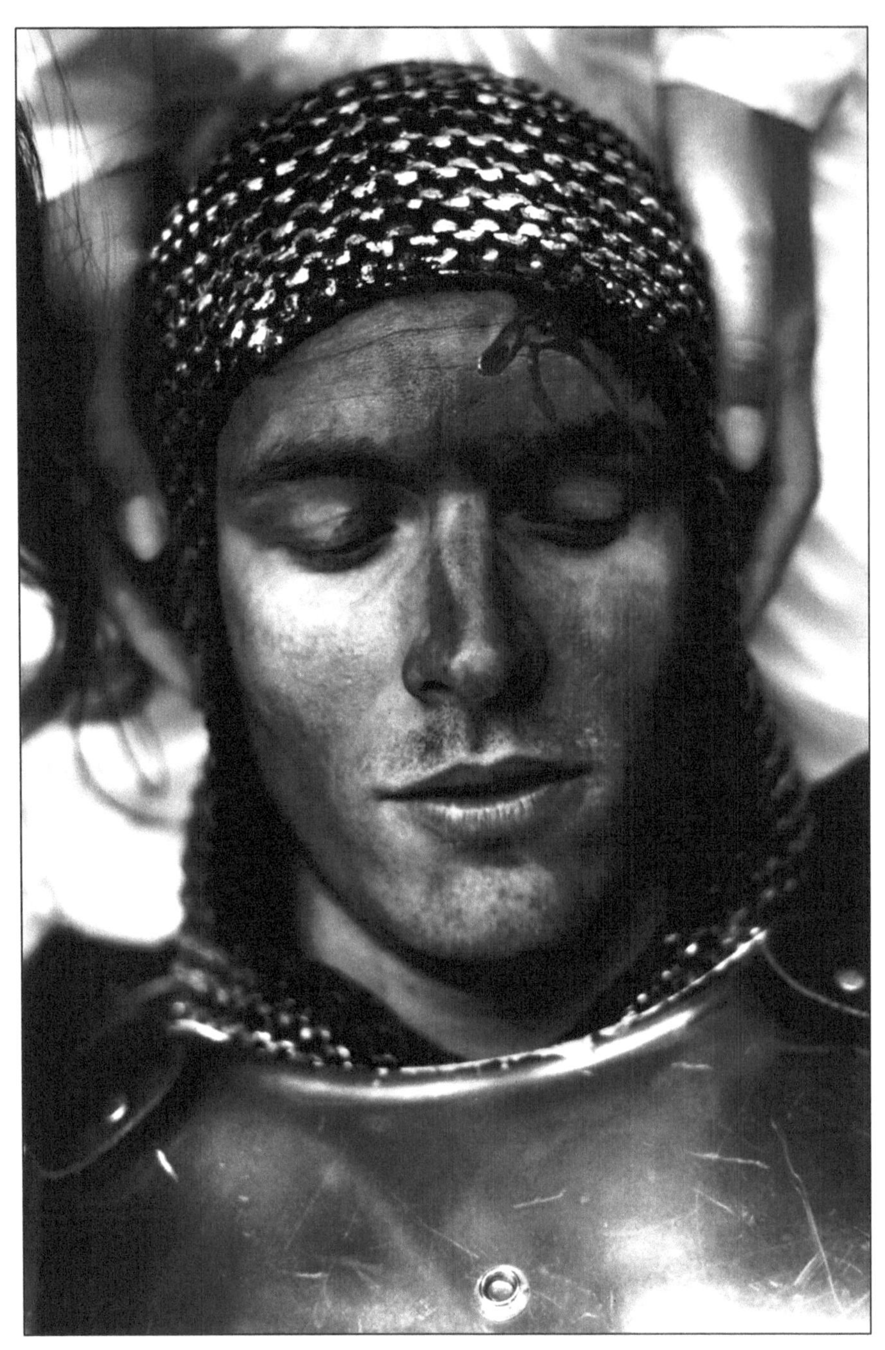

And slowly answered Arthur from the barge:
'The old order changeth, yielding place to new,
And God fulfils Himself in many ways,
Lest one good custom should corrupt the world.
Comfort thyself: what comfort is in me?
I have lived my life, and that which I have done
May He within Himself make pure!

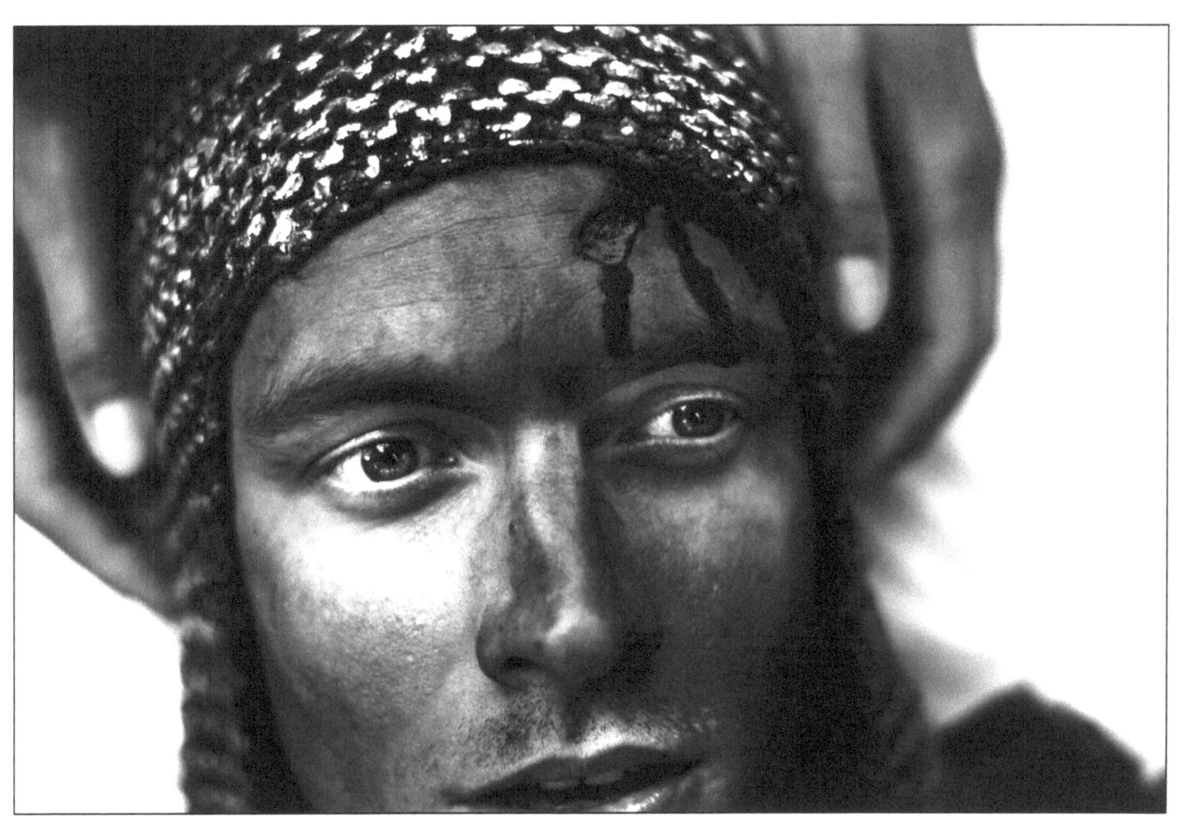

But now farewell. I am going a long way
With these thou seëst-if indeed I go-
(For all my mind is clouded with a doubt)
To the island-valley of Avilion;
Where falls not hail, or rain, or any snow,
Nor ever wind blows loudly; but it lies
Deep-meadow'd, happy, fair with orchard-lawns
And bowery hollows crown'd with summer sea,
Where I will heal me of my grievous wound.'

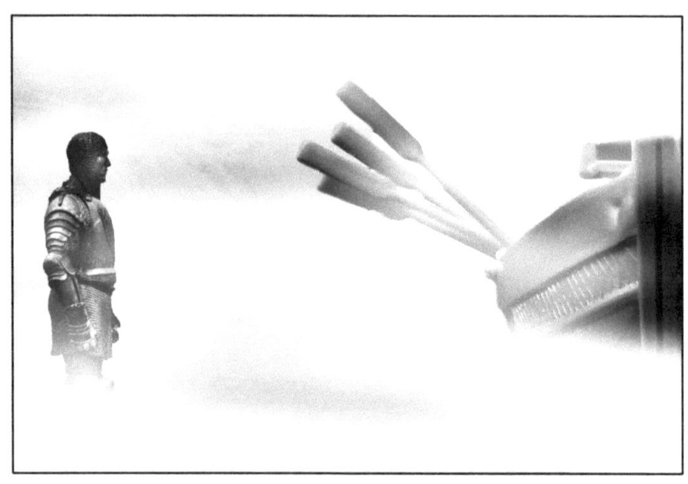

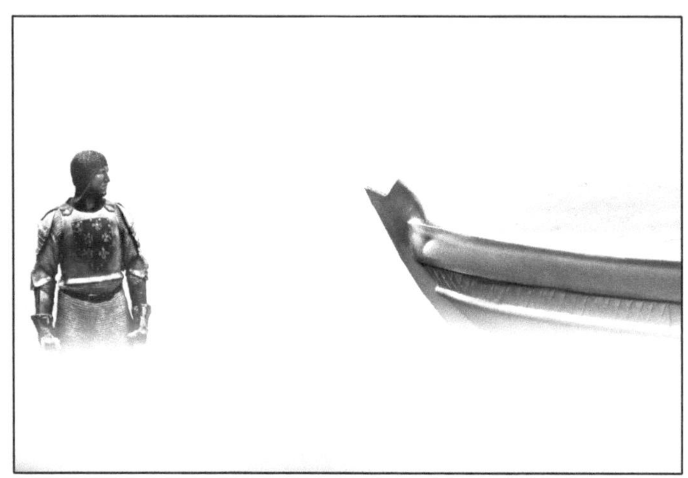

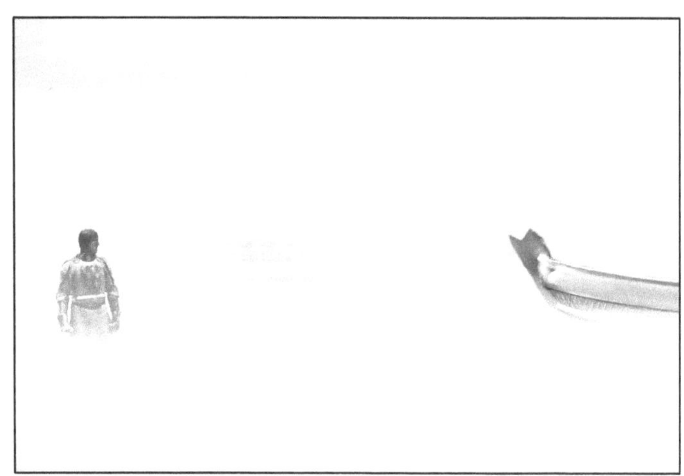

So said he, and the barge with oar and sail
Moved from the brink, like some full-breasted swan
That, fluting a wild carol ere here death,
Ruffles her pure cold plume, and takes the flood with swarthy webs.

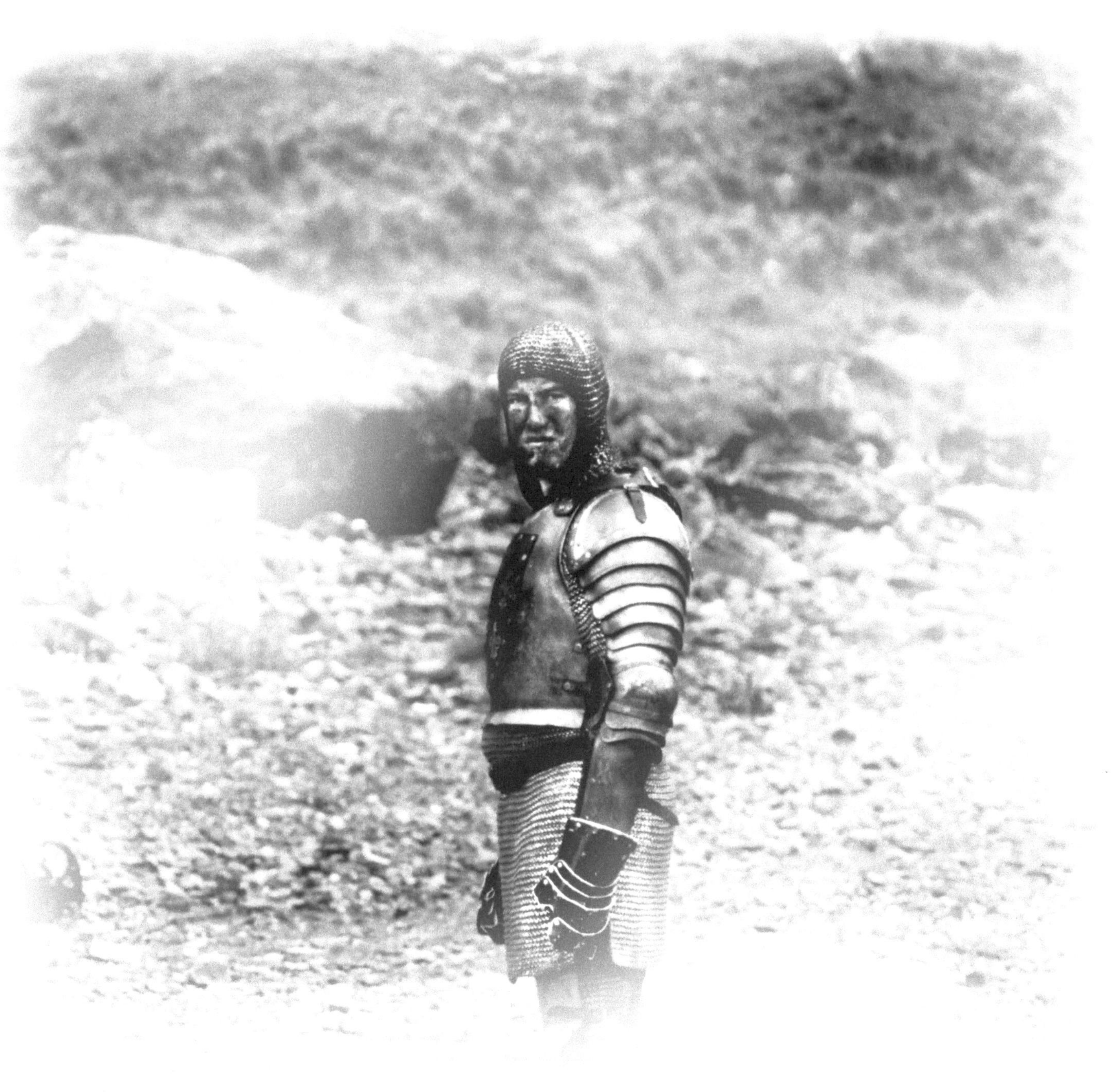

Long stood Sir Bedivere
Revolving many memories...

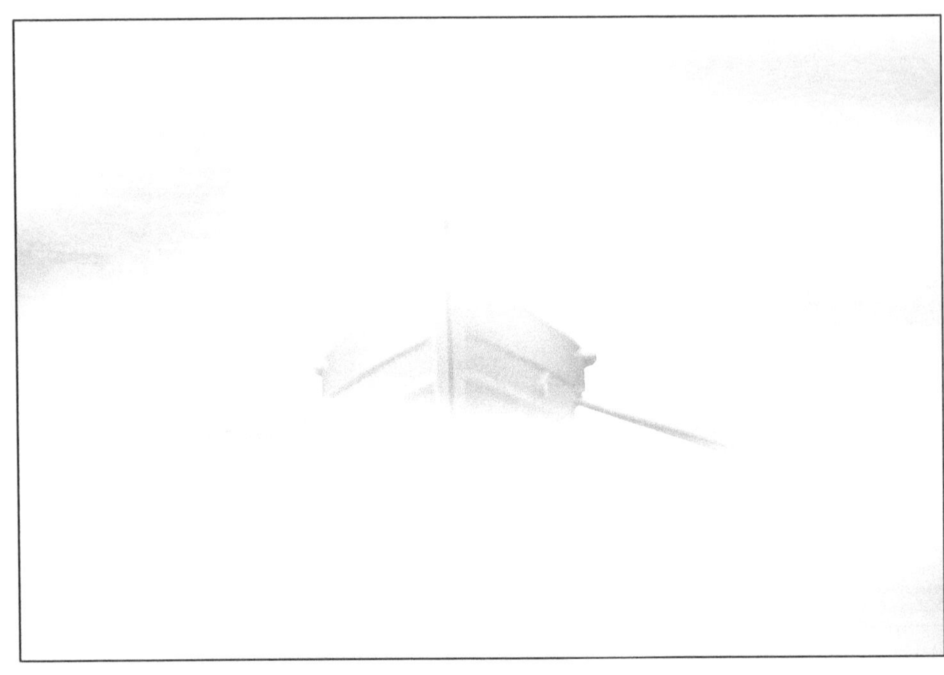

Till the hull look'd one black dot against the verge of dawn,
And on the mere the wailing died away.

The End...

(for now)

Arthur shall return...

The Exhibition

Following the completion of this two year project, I was fortunate that several outside individuals took a strong interest in the work, resulting in an exhibition held at the aptly named King Arthur Hotel, located on the Gower Peninsula in South Wales.
The opening of the exhibition was attended by over one hundred people, who were witness to King Arthur himself making an appearence . The following pages contain examples of the promotional graphics used for the run up to the exhibition, including the private invitation which can be seen below.

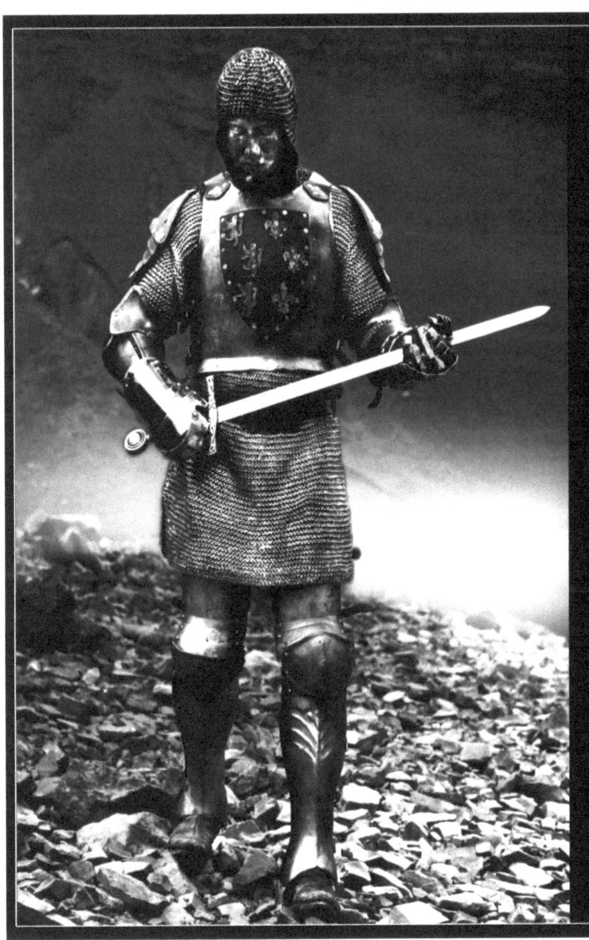

A Unique Exhibition

Neil Collier *BSc. A.B.I.P.P. Q.E.P.*

A photographic representation of
Alfred Lord Tennyson's 'Morte d'Arthur'

Invitation to the Private Viewing
At the King Arthur Hotel,
Reynoldston, Gower, Swansea
20th January 2005, 6pm

Guest speaker - Professor Terry Stevens

Buffet and Wine

Neil Collier BSc. A.B.I.P.P. Q.E.P.

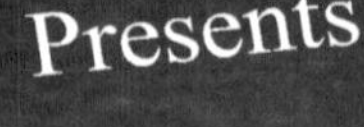

A Unique Exhibition

A photographic
representation of
Alfred Lord Tennyson's
'Morte d'Arthur'

Here at The
King Arthur Hotel
Friday January 21st
-Sunday 23rd
2005

Opening Times
1.30pm until 9pm
Free Entry

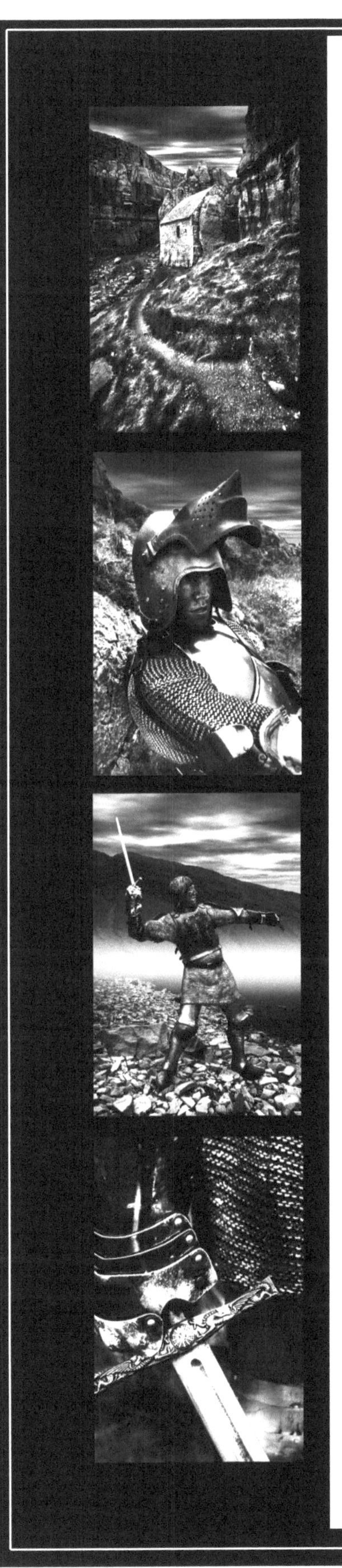

Neil Collier BSc. A.B.I.P.P Q.E.P

A Unique Exhibition...

A Photographic
Representation of
Alfred Lord Tennyson's
'Morte d'Arthur'

Here at The
King Arthur Hotel
Friday January 21st
-Sunday 23rd
2005

Opening Times
1.30pm - 9pm
Free Entry

Ninety-two Images
Portraying Arthur's
Final Command &
The Start of His long
Journey to Avalon...

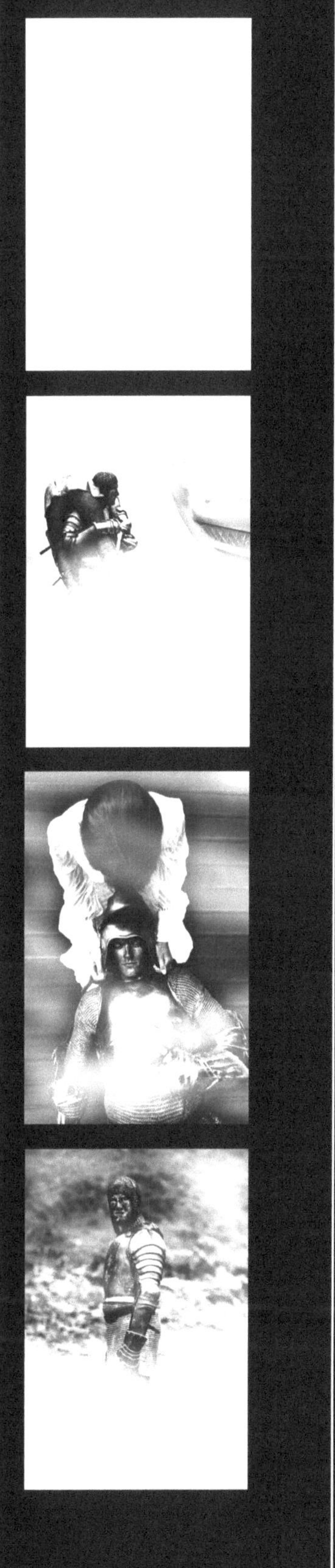

Meet the Team

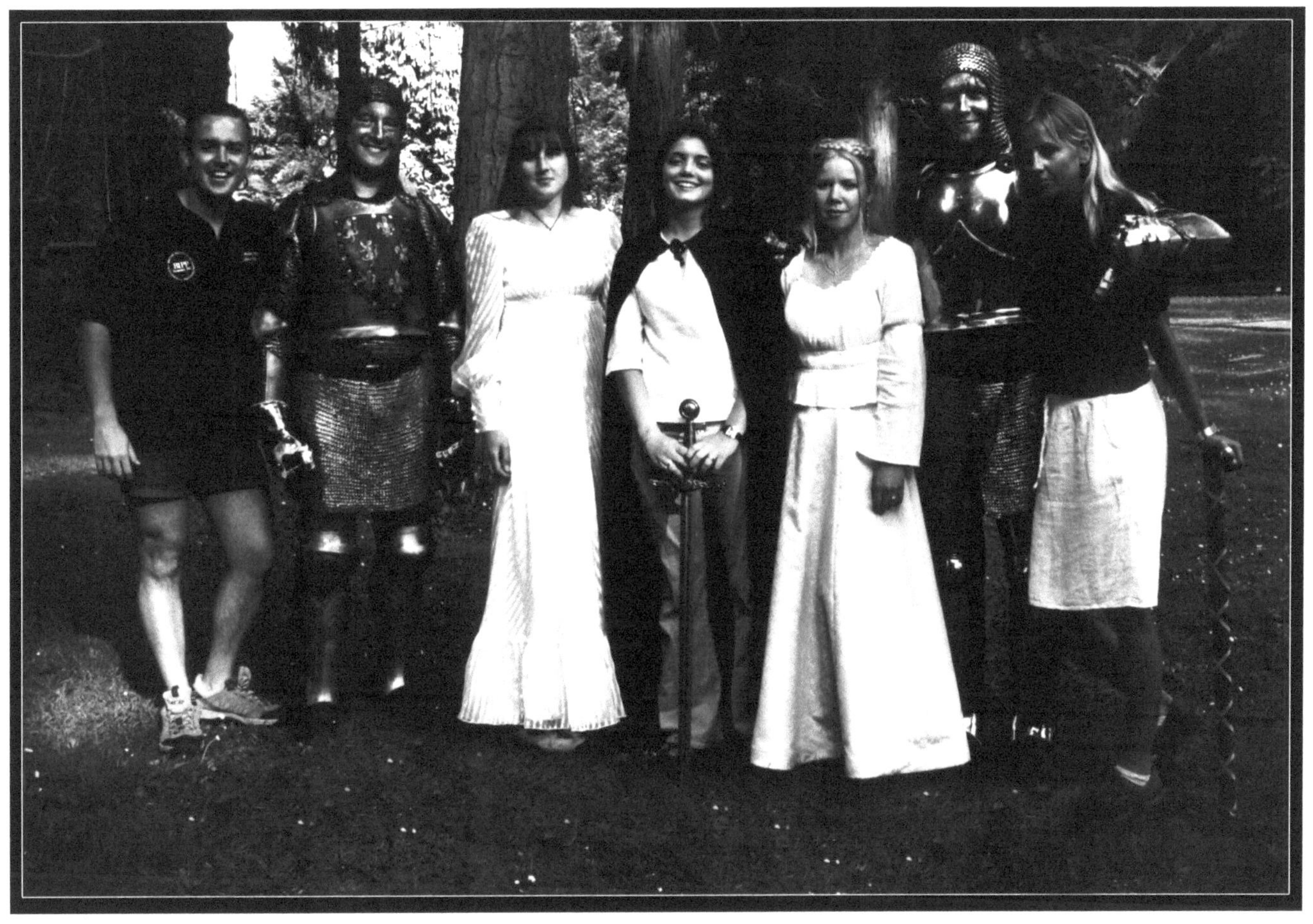

I would like to take this opportunity again to thank six wonderful people who gave up a lot of time to bring this project to life. Without them I would not have been able to complete the task at hand.

From left to right:

Me, Martin, Wendy, Laura, Sillé, Grant and Helen.

Thanks again.

Locations of Legend

All photography for this project was carried out at three significant locations in South Wales. The first of these was Llyn Y Fan Fach reservoir in the Black Mountains, which has Welsh links to the Arthurian legends, in addition to local lore of actual healers who once lived in the vacinity of the reservoirs. One cannot describe the beauty of this location and I would recommend anyone to visit.

The second key location was Carreg Cennen Castle in Trapp, near Llandeilo. The first journey towards the castle on the thin country road will be one of the most memorable. High up on a rocky throne sits this wonderful castle, its attached myth claims that King Arthur and his knights lie asleep, awaiting the day when Britain needs them again.

Finally, there is the Gower Peninsula, the first ever recorded area of outstanding natural beauty. At the top of Cefn Bryn, located approximately in the middle of the peninsula lies Arthur's Stone which is supposed to have come to rest there after King Arthur dislodged it from his shoe and threw it on the journey to his final battle at Camlaan.

www.ingramcontent.com/pod-product-compliance
Ingram Content Group UK Ltd.
Pitfield, Milton Keynes, MK11 3LW, UK
UKHW060121300726
14090UKWH00002B/294
* 9 7 8 0 9 5 5 8 4 8 7 0 4 *